LILI DEBARBIERI

SEDONA VERDE VALLEY
ART

A HISTORY *from* RED ROCKS *to* PLEIN-AIR

THE
History
PRESS

Published by The History Press
Charleston, SC 29403
www.historypress.net

Front cover, center: Betty Carr. *Morning at Jerome.* Oil on canvas. *Artist's collection.*

First published 2015

Manufactured in the United States

ISBN 978.1.62619.841.8

Library of Congress Control Number: 2014959949

CONTENTS

Acknowledgements   5
Introduction   7

1. Places of Beauty: Inspiration
   in the High Desert   11
2. It's an Artist's World Out There   17
3. The Verde Valley   27
4. Portraits of the Artists   49
5. Patrons and Artists   95

Afterword   101
A Guide to Galleries   103
Bibliography   107
Index   109
About the Author   112

Acknowledgements

I would like to express a special heartfelt thank-you and my eternal gratitude to the following organizations and people for sharing their enthusiasm, feedback, tremendous support and expertise during the writing stages of this book: the Sedona Historical Society, Jerome Historical Society, Arizona Historical Society, Visit Sedona, the Phoenix Art Museum, the Sedona Art Museum, Sedona Center for the Arts, Jerome Arts Cooperative, the Tucson Museum of Art Research Library and the Sedona Public Library, Janeen Trevillyan, Donna Chesler, Linda Goldstein, Julee Cohen, Terrie Frankel and Diane Sward Rapaport. To the artists themselves—Jan Sitts, Birgitta Lapides, Cody DeLong, Dave Santillanes, Ellen J.D. Roberts, Joella Jean Mahoney, Betty and Howard Carr, Bernie Lopez, Quang Huang, John Soderberg, Mark Rownd, Bill Nebeker, John Coleman, Curt Walters and John and Ruth Waddell—I will be forever grateful for your trust, insights and participation.

INTRODUCTION

On a school assignment for an introductory class to art history, I sip a huge cappuccino at the New York City's Metropolitan Museum of Art while taking notes on Rembrandt's style and technique. This memory is particularly present whenever I reflect on my experiences of art. The memories come in pieces and fragments, as most memories often do; early experiences from childhood are the most striking—my parents were both artists. I still adore the watercolor illustrations of Beatrix Potter as much as her stories. I think of pieces and places I've been over the years. At the Pennsylvania Academy of Fine Arts, a simple winter scene, the Impressionist masters on view in Paris, the recycled art of Cape Town or the murals of Tucson. I find myself filled with these snapshots of memories over the years reflecting on a lifelong interest and academic aptitude for the subject of art history.

Like the words a person uses to tell a story, a painter uses brushes and paints not to simply define a form but also to convey a mood or feeling. I am sure this is why the visual arts have a way of affecting our lives in such singular ways. Art has brought much beauty, tranquility when needed and even meaning into different periods of my own life. A painting illuminates the drabbest of rooms; a sculpture transforms the grimiest of city parks. Whether we are creating, viewing or supporting, life is transformed by these mediums.

Seeking a common element, a pattern or blueprint to articulate what unites the members of Sedona's community of artists, I began this project. If there are two commonalities present, it is a diversity that defies categorization and the structures and organizations that support and nourish these artists. It is the Sedona Arts Center.

Located just on the outskirts of the never-ceasing hustle and bustle of Uptown Sedona, this is a calming, unassuming historic structure that exudes tranquility and serves as a mecca for area, regional and far-flung artists. The communal focal point packs a big punch for its relatively small space and is distinctive architecturally. It is in the foothills with towering red rocks overhead.

The exhibit I am in town to see on this clear fall day is titled "Max Ernst: From Surrealist to Abstract." As you walk into the art barn, the painting by Ernst's wife, Surrealist painter Dorothea Tanning, titled *Birthday* immediately catches my eye. The painting was so titled by Ernst. I am greeted by the show's gregarious host, art collector and exhibiting Abstract painter himself, Mark Rownd. Rownd is a fascinating wealth of information about this little-known and under-appreciated period in Sedona's art history.

Birthday is the painting that made Tanning a leading Surrealist painter. It is almost impossible to take my eyes away from this piece. A documentary is showing as well titled *Max Ernst Hanging*. I peruse a copy of Tanning's autobiography as well as a biography of Peggy Guggenheim. "Max Ernst was a kind of 'Founding Father of Modern Art,'" says Rownd. "As the story goes, it was Ernst who taught Pollock drip painting."

The show traces the development of Max Ernst as an artist over the decades. I survey Ernst's work from each decade of the early twentieth century along with a *Life* magazine spread of Ernst and Tanning in Sedona. Along with *Birthday*, the most fascinating pieces are Ernst's miniatures, created during the artist's tenure in Sedona. At first, it seems that the miniatures are merely smaller copies of larger paintings, but this is not so. They are really just that: original miniature paintings, often no larger than postage stamps, created with a magnifying glass by Ernst. Prior to his move to Sedona in 1947, Ernst painted huge landscapes of eroded earth in Paris. Ironically, in this oft-described larger-than-life landscape, Ernst chose to create miniature works. Ernst equipped them with Surrealist titles meant to suggest what he sees in the picture. For example, a red blob (on a white background) suggested a song to the artist, so he called his painting *Love Song on a Snow Bed*. As a means of relaxation from painting microbes, Ernst liked to carve monster-sized sculptures made out of cement and pumice that he affectionately identified as family and placed at the fringe of his garden in Sedona.

I return to the Ernst exhibit the following day, so inspired by Ernst and Tanning's life, work and times, for one last look. With the chatter of a lively group of German tourists in the background, I gaze on Rownd's Abstract paintings *Desert Music* (at the other end of the exhibit space), *Time Squared* and *Rhythm Painting*, wishing I could remain in this world of art on the outskirts of big-city Arizona.

The state as a whole has attracted those in the visual arts from its earliest days as a place of human settlement. Arizona's artistic legacy predates statehood, U.S. territorial status and Mexican and Spanish rule. It began with the prehistoric native populations of the Anastasi and Hohokum in the form of the petroglyphs and pictographs or "rock art"—images incised or painted on the surface of rocks. These evocative images include those of human-like forms, plants, animals and abstract and geometric configurations. They enchanted artists and travelers who were and continue to be drawn here, including the illustrators attached to early government survey parties. At first, artists appeared in Arizona as straightforward chroniclers and then as illustrators. Finally, they assumed the position of creators of fine art and thus the modern tradition of drawing and painting in Arizona was born. Indeed, few states, outside the population hub of the Northeast, can claim to be represented by so extensive and diverse an array of varied artists, including Maxfield Parrish, David Hockney and Jackson Pollock. Most notably, the state has influenced the development of the western art movement in the United States.

The Sedona Verde Valley region is a place where art has particularly flourished and thrived. It seems timely to envision a book that reflects what we know of the area's art history and its artists, and I soon sharpened my focus to a few mediums of painting, sculpture and mixed media. My aim in writing this book was to explore how the area's artists have used the experience of the western landscape in their art. How do they respond to and interpret the issues in the West? What role do they play in their communities? Which artists and periods of art history have in turn inspired their work? What keeps them going as professionals and people?

I chose to focus on the Verde Valley region not only because of the incomparable natural beauty here but also because of the integration of art into virtually every part of the city from galleries to eateries and public attractions and from private homes to nonprofit organizations. In short, the town oozes the aesthetic in every aspect of daily life for its residents and visitors. In the bright mixed media of Jan Sitts, the unforgettable bronze historical sculpture of John Coleman and the life-affirming landscape paintings of Joella Jean Mahoney, among so many others, each artist I had the pleasure of knowing effortlessly reflected his or her own work—they are present in their art much like a writer is present in what he or she writes. Through the following works, the story of a place is revealed, too.

PLACES OF BEAUTY

INSPIRATION IN THE HIGH DESERT

Everywhere you go, a panorama of natural beauty surrounds you—cliffs; a sea of greens, pinks and reds of every shade; and public art installations along each stretch of road. The smell of pine permeates the air; even in summer there is a cool breeze. Folks here are friendly and unguarded and proud of being outside big-city Arizona.

From the exotic and aesthetic to kitsch, Sedona has it all. Over 50 percent of Sedona is privately owned, and the rest is Coconino National Forest, all situated at a cool 4,500 feet. In this desert town, to value aesthetic beauty is a way of life. The buildings here are all lovely earth tones, and even the local McDonald's goes without its golden arches in favor of a more southwestern teal green mandated by city ordinance so as not to detract from the natural beauty of the area. Frank Lloyd Wright protégé and master of mid-twentieth-century modern architecture Howard Madole was Sedona's first architect. Madole designed homes in town that still have a following, including the Rigby House, Madole House and several along Madole Drive, many of which are protected and preserved.

During the 1970s, a pilgrimage of New Age folks migrated to Sedona from California; 64 percent of visitors to the town still come for spiritual reasons. Here it is fine and dandy to be weird; this is a place to reflect, to sit and just be, to meditate. The movie set caught the fever, too, and Sedona can claim Al Pacino, Sharon Stone and Nicholas Cage as residents.

I spent the summer of 2014 touring Taos, New Mexico, a city world famous for its art community and architecture. Sedona's infrastructure and offerings seemed comparatively more impressive somehow: clean streets, sidewalks everywhere, impeccable grand and historic homes, a local bus system and every type of food and arts institutions available (except an art museum, but more on that omission later).

CHAPEL OF THE HOLY CROSS

Overlooking this beautiful display of an art town sits the Chapel of the Holy Cross, one of the most incredible churches in the world, certainly in this country. No services are currently held here. The residential area beneath the chapel is simply called "Chapel" and is home to some of the most impressive real estate in the country, the grandest of which is the estate of a billionaire Romanian inventor, Sedona's answer to William Randolph Hearst. The property even boasts two indoor swimming pools filled with fish. Yes, Sedona is a very rich locale.

In these hills, Marguerite Brunswig Staude, an heiress and an artist, dreamed of building a chapel shaped like a cross. Staude's family fled Europe before the Holocaust, and as a young woman, Staude studied art and sculpture in France and Italy. Seeing the Empire State Building during its construction, she was inspired to build a modern Catholic chapel. With the help of Barry Goldwater, land in Sedona's Little Horse Park was allocated for construction. Legend has it that Staude chose the location for the church because she saw a pharmaceutical symbol in the rock. She deemed this a sign, as her father had been a druggist. But it turns out that homesteader Lee Roy Piper's brand was "Rx," and he had carved the symbol on the rock. After Marguerite married Tony Staude in 1938, the couple lived in Sedona. The Chapel of the Holy Cross was completed in 1956. This beautiful spiritual tourist attraction is now administered by the Roman Catholic Church.

Surrounded by red rocks and green pine forest, the place is very much in harmony with its environment. The chapel itself belies the opulence of the surrounding homes with its simple, small wood benches. The real worship going on here is of God's magnificent red rock creation visible all around the structure and through its large glass windows. Although architects designed the chapel, Marguerite herself built the Madonna sculpture inside and designed its Stations of the Cross.

I light a candle here for the first time in years. I gaze at the distinctive sculptures and features inside this religious structure unlike any I've ever seen:

an archangel Michael hand carved and gilded; the head of Christ in granite from Chartres, France; and many pieces created by Marguerite herself. The place is described as a "modern" Catholic church and is on the National Register of Historic Places. It is one manifestation and representation of Sedona's spiritual pull.

TLAQUEPAQUE ARTS AND CRAFTS VILLAGE

After spending the morning at the Chapel of the Holy Cross, I make my way to another place with a spiritual pull in its own right—Tlaquepaque Arts and Crafts Village. The arts village is immediately noticeable as one of the most distinctive architectural gems here. It is a cool oasis along a creek with ivy-covered walls and bubbling fountains. You feel like you are walking back in time; I overhear many folks say this must have been a monastery, but it was in fact built in the 1970s. Truly, the place recalls colonial Mexico—there is a remarkable Old World feeling at Tlaquepaque, and even the name rolls off your tongue pleasantly. With no direct path to one location or courtyard, the village enchants me in a few short minutes, and its sycamores and vegetation create the desire to meander and discover.

It all began when its founder, successful Nevada businessman Abe Miller, began coming to Sedona on vacations. He fell in love with the town, as the story goes, and specifically with this creek-side property. It was conceived to build a place reflecting the charm and mood of old Mexico, another travel favorite. Sedona was a natural location for a living village where artisans work in full view and are able to live on site, as a complement to the Sedona Arts Center located near the village. Miller called it Tlaquepaque (an ancient Aztec word that means the "best of everything") after the colorful Mexican city on the outskirts of Guadalajara. Miller was ordered to not tear down any sycamore in the sycamore grove of the property as a condition of buying the land. Truckloads of iron grillwork, giant carved doors, handmade lanterns, clay pots and benches soon were coming from Mexico into Sedona on a regular basis, creating the genuine feel and spirit of Tlaquepaque that has remained. Miller died just a few months after construction was completed; he spent almost ten years of his life realizing this arts and crafts village.

Today, you will find great sycamore limbs merging with rooflines, growing through massive walls. After years of growth, Tlaquepaque is graced with climbing vines of sweet-scented honeysuckle, purple clematis, ivy trumpet vine and silver lace. Pansies are everywhere in early spring and remain until late April, when the Arizona sun becomes too strong for their survival. This was not conceived as a purely commercial venture, which made it incredibly special.

I take a break in the chapel area of Tlaquepaque, listening to the sound of water and crickets. The small chapel was Miller's favorite building, and he often spent time there. He commissioned Eileen Conn to create a painting of St. Augustine, Pope Pius X, St. Bonaventure, Samuel, Peter and John the Baptist that is resplendently set off in a beautiful gold-leaf frame painted by Abe and Linn Miller. The chapel is a place of serenity in the midst of the liveliness and bustle of Tlaquepaque. The chapel was designed as a place for meditation and contemplation.

Considered by many a local to be the "art and soul of Sedona," the village of today not only supports world-class galleries but also supports Sedona's not-for-profit organizations attempting to create "cultural events that not only fit within the theme of Tlaquepaque but also help support the general economy of Sedona," says general manager Wendy Lippman. The Marigold Project is a classic event that demonstrates the community's commitment to the arts. The project is a public mural for which townsfolk are invited to paint and create something for a loved one of the past.

THE HOUSE OF SEVEN ARCHES

Above the village is another singular architectural gem. Throughout literary history, Gothic Revival–style homes have captured our imaginations. Sedona has its own version of a mysterious house on the hill with its own charismatic context: the House of Seven Arches.

Sedona's House of Seven Arches was originally built in 1978 by architectural visionary Herb Winebarger. The house is a steel-and-wood construction perched dramatically on the side of a steep mountain, high above other buildings in Sedona that are intentionally low lying. Herb sold the home to a member of Lucille Ball's family. The grand home is four thousand square feet with two thousand square feet of covered wraparound decks and two fireplaces, five bedrooms, four baths and a large spa.

For over thirty years, tourists and locals have referred to the home as Lucy's House, although no concrete evidence exists that Lucille Ball ever lived in the home. Nevertheless, to this day, a mannequin resembling Lucille Ball can be seen on the balcony. Lucille's family believes that at one time, she owned the entire hillside, as she purchased lots of property in the area when she divorced Desi Arnaz. Lucy and her brother, Fred Ball, individually owned several properties in the surrounding area. Fred Ball helped Lucy during her early career in Hollywood and managed the Desi Arnaz Indian Wells Resort, where Lucy's piano resided.

Terrie Frankel, a former Doublemint twin, purchased the house over twenty years ago and has lived there with her twin sister, Jennie, for many years. "In 1992, Jennie purchased a home in the Village of Oak Creek. I was living in Los Angeles at the time. I drove from LA with Jennie to bring some of her furniture here. We drove down from Flagstaff and I was amazed at the beauty of Oak Creek Canyon. Jennie said, 'You haven't seen anything yet!' We were at the bridge beneath this House of Seven Arches and I looked up from the car, pointed to the house and said, 'I want to meet the people who own that house some day!'" said Terrie. Little did Terrie know that mere years later, she would meet the man who owned the house, have a book on the *New York Times* bestsellers list (*You'll Never Make Love in this Town Again*) and end up owning the intriguing home.

When Frankel first moved to Sedona, there was only one stoplight in Uptown. She quickly fell in love with living in the area, telling people enthusiastically, "I ran out of places to pinch myself. The views are spectacular and I've put an Earth Cam on my balcony so that people all over the world can enjoy them," she said.

Colored lights that Terrie changes to match holidays illuminate the arches at night. Inside the house, you see photographs of the twins' USO tour of Vietnam, as well as Terri's "Wall of Fame," featuring photographs with movie stars from their days in Hollywood. (Jennie was an Emmy judge, and Terrie was on the board of directors of the Producers Guild of America.)

Terri cherishes the memories of sharing her home with her twin sister, which include recently purchasing Lucille Ball's piano from Lucy's nephew, Geoffrey Ball, an architectural designer who worked on the home, and sharing their home with guests from China (this Renaissance woman speaks Cantonese and Mandarin). Terrie is somewhat eccentrically known for having Lucille Ball birthday parties that are a media favorite. Lucy's 100th Birthday Party was in 2011.

Among those who created the architectural wonders and public art pieces of Sedona, Frankel is one who has given much to this high desert community, the least of which is the organization Gardens for Humanity.

The organization was founded by author, artist, poet and activist Adele Seronde herself, who was passionate about creating beauty and community through art and horticulture. Seronde previously served as a coordinator of the visual arts for Boston's Summerthing, the city's neighborhood arts program dedicated to humanizing city environments through the arts and community participation.

The organization's current president, Richard Sidy, was searching for an opportunity that would be as exciting as his profession as educator. He wanted to connect with people and help them learn more about environmental stewardship, gardening and their connection to nature. "I had been an organic gardener for some forty years and had been involved in starting community gardens in Los Angeles in the 1970s. Gardens for Humanity bring together like-minded creative people to improve the environment and the quality of life for people," said Sidy.

In the organization's impressive first ten years, twenty-eight gardens were built, catalyzed and/or funded in four states in urban and rural places of need, in schools and healthcare facilities and on reservations. Later, the organization's projects involved partnerships with the Sedona public schools and the Institute of Eco-Tourism to initiate a Hopi-Sedona exchange student program in sharing reciprocal cultures through arts and gardening. In the past few years, Gardens for Humanity has shifted its focus to education and implemented a greater emphasis on school gardens, art and environmental and community education. The gardens in Sedona and elsewhere are venues for aesthetic appreciation and contemplation. Healing and regaining a connection to the natural world took on a greater context with Gardens for Humanity as an essential part of healing the planet.

Many of Gardens for Humanity's most ardent supporters are Sedona's artists and art organizations that have been instrumental in developing the educational program called "Celebrating the Art in Earth," funded by the Arizona Commission on the Arts. This enrichment program uses art to teach about the environment and gardening while providing much-needed art education and aesthetic understanding.

"Art, as the means of environmental and garden education, helps students develop greater self-expression, creativity, experimentation, problem solving, in addition to enhancing their emotional relationship, appreciation and sense of responsibility towards the natural world," affirms Sidy. This groundbreaking organization ensures that future generations of the area are nurtured and transformed by the beauty of natural places as well as human creations.

2

IT'S AN ARTIST'S WORLD
OUT THERE

The region of the Southwestern United States and Arizona in particular, brings much opportunity for any lover of the visual arts. For the past century or more, the state has attracted and retained an astounding number of the creatively inclined. Though many aspects of Arizona's history and geography have influenced explorers, homesteaders and artists, one aspect seems to transcend medium and time period: the landscape. One of the most multifaceted destinations in the world, the Arizona landscape, both the natural experiences with and the internal interpretations of, has been a catalyst of inspiration to generations of artists. The area's vast and charismatic deserts, majestic mountains and dense forests impact the imagination and output of myriad artists. Something truly extraordinary in the air conspires in a way to concoct the wildest of creations.

The en plein-air (French for "in open air") technique of landscape painting advocates close observation of nature, but the phrase can have a broader meaning. Plein-air refers not only to landscapes that were painted on location outdoors but also studio works closely based on nature observed firsthand.

Plein-air painters do not merely copy their subjects but enhance their appearance in ways so subtle that the viewer is mesmerized by the artist's interpretation of nature. During the early nineteenth century, by sketching en plein-air, landscape painters could work with greater spontaneity and immediacy. During this period, artists's works reflected the importance of daily life and immersion in nature, and so the open-air sketch acquired a new and greater significance.

Sketching outdoors became a wildly popular, almost scientific pursuit, earnestly endeavored to study firsthand the diversity of natural phenomena and the ephemeral appearances of landscapes. In painting the trunk of a tree, a single flower, a riverbank, a cloud or the accidental effects of light and shade, there was an authenticity, artists claimed, that arose from the eye rather than the mind. This movement was a dramatic departure from the classical notion of art in which human reason and intellect are central.

By the 1820s, the practice of open-air sketching had become widespread in Europe, and by the later part of the century, most famously realized in French Impressionism, the open-air sketch became an autonomous style of art. On the other side of the Atlantic, a romance was growing out of Americans' relationship to the land and their accomplishments within it. It was this Romantic imagery that pushed Americans farther and farther west. Beginning with the Lewis and Clark Expedition in 1804, the U.S. government began sponsoring probing adventures into its vast western territories. These served many purposes: negotiating with Native American tribes, exploring the best routes for travel, cataloging the native flora and fauna, meticulously examining the land's geological reserves and finally issuing richly illustrated reports of these investigative odysseys. As information from the journeys accumulated, their numbers increased dramatically.

Then, in 1821, the Santa Fe Trail was established between Missouri and New Mexico. In 1843, a thousand settlers departed from Independence, Missouri, for the Oregon Territory, marking the beginning of the great homesteading movement influencing the development of American art. As national frontiers opened and expanded, nineteenth-century Americans yearned for knowledge about their rapidly growing country and its richly diverse parts. The public was particularly hungry for images of the land, its mountains, forests and prairies; the lives and customs of the Native Americans who dwelt on it; and the adventurous men and women who moved into and settled it. Seeking illumination about the Southwest, one of the last in this country's mysterious and exotic places, Americans turned to the work of pioneering artists—their only source for reliable visual impressions of these hitherto foreign lands. Through plein-air paintings and sketches, Americans learned of this new land, and artists built careers. While in the early nineteenth century American culture was still as rooted as ever in its European heritage, there was nevertheless a unique quality about this land that was recognized by Americans and Europeans alike as distinctly American.

Soon after the acquisition of the Arizona Territory from Mexico in 1848, the U.S. government's survey parties and soldier-explorers of the U.S. Army's Corp of Topographical Engineers entered the region accompanied by artists for the express purpose of landscape painting and open-air sketching. Beginning with General Stephen Watts Kearny's march from Santa Fe to San Diego in 1846, Arizona was continually crisscrossed for the next four decades in order to document possible rail routes, mineral wealth deposits, town sites and water sources. Most of these surveys included accompanying U.S. government–employed artists who helped narrate this epic of national discovery.

There was no greater prototype of a survey artist than John Mix Stanley. Stanley traveled with Kearny's expedition as a topographer, becoming the first non–Native American artist to visit Arizona. General Kearny was en route to San Diego to help defend the United States during the Mexican War. Kearny was in command of a small group charged to traverse the region to San Diego in order to defend and secure California from the Mexican government, an action that eventually dictated the final borders of the Southwest. His duty was to visually report what the landscape and its inhabitants looked like for inclusion in a published government report following completion of the expedition.

Stanley's detailed and exact art was in stark contrast to early twentieth-century painters, who were commissioned by the Santa Fe Railroad to paint the Grand Canyon and the Native Americans of northern Arizona in such a way as to encourage tourism to the West. The artist's work was intended for lithographic reproduction when the report of the expedition was published. Stanley's published lithographs included predominantly geological subjects and biological specimen illustrations. Illustrations such as these augmented the impact of government reports because verbal descriptions of newly discovered plants, such as the saguaro and cholla, were inadequate, to say the least, and often incomprehensible to eastern Washington-based officials.

Twenty years later, incandescent landscape painter Thomas Moran was summoned to the West for Major John W. Powell's third trip through the Grand Canyon in 1873. Known as the father of Grand Canyon exploration, Powell was the first American to travel the length of the canyon by way of the Colorado River. He had returned on several occasions to understand more completely this geological wonderland, realizing that if he were to emphasize in Washington the importance of his geologic studies of the site, he must provide a visual—"the landscape is too vast, too complex, and too grand for verbal description."

In 1873, Powell requested that Moran accompany him to the Grand Canyon. The previous year, Moran had painted the huge canvas *Grand Canyon of the Yellowstone*, which hung in the Senate lobby. This grand picture was a spectacular success. Born in England and raised in Philadelphia, Moran had no formal training in art. He began his career as a watercolorist, and his fresh, quick strokes and light translucent color carried over into his work in oil. Moran's large picture was painted in 1872, the same year Congress established Yellowstone National Park. In it, he demonstrated that the American school of landscape painting had matured to a point that the painter's concern was as much with the painterly effects of art as with the depiction of nature. Hence, in about 1870, a major shift in American painting commenced.

Moran continued the great panoramic landscape tradition, frequently painting on canvases that measured twelve feet across, writing, "I have always held that the grandest, most beautiful, or wonderful in nature, would, in capable hands, make the grandest, most beautiful, or wonderful pictures."

Moran carries us into an American West of magnificent mountain ranges and sublime valleys and canyons. The result of Moran's trip to Arizona was his painting the *Chasm of the Colorado* (1874), which aimed to bring before the public the character of that region. The painting was then also hung in the Senate lobby by the Yellowstone picture.

Moran's name soon became nearly synonymous with the Grand Canyon. The artist is most often credited with introducing this geologic wonder to the American public and for influencing a generation of artists to re-create it in his style during the following years. During the next fifty years, Moran traveled western America and visited the Grand Canyon and its environs on a number of occasions. A prolific painter, he completed scores of works with little stylistic changes over the years—a detailed foreground for vast landscapes, utilizing the expedition photographs of the survey photographers.

In many ways, Stanley and Moran bridged the world of art intended for specific scientific purposes and that of works made for the sake of providing illustrations to a wider audience. American appetites were whetted by these works, and East Coast publishers began to commission work. The ensuing golden age of American illustration, which lasted from the mid-1870s through the first decade of the twentieth century, was fueled by accounts of frontier events taking place in the imaginations of creative writers and in the western territories. From this era came artists who desired to paint Arizona for personal reasons rather than as an assignment. Arizona became better known to the public because of these artists, and many of the artists became better known because of their paintings of Arizona.

Thereafter, and for many years to come, the focus of the development of Arizona art turned to the reporter-artists with Frederick Remington as a quintessential example. Though Moran is synonymous with the Grand Canyon, Frederic Remington's name is synonymous with art of the American West. His first true masterpiece, *A Dash for the Timber* (1889), was roughly based on his earlier experiences in Arizona and led to a number of works that same year with Arizona and Mexico as subject matter.

Remington had always been drawn toward military subjects and lifestyles. The artist traveled to Montana, Arizona, New Mexico and Texas. He wandered, he looked, he studied and he sketched. When he returned to Kansas City, he had a huge portfolio of simple but forceful drawings. He took them to New York, and Harper and Outing bought the sketches as magazine illustrations. When Teddy Roosevelt started his great book *Ranch Life and the Hunting Trail*, he selected Remington to illustrate it, a joint venture that paid dividends many times over for the artist.

Remington's reputation rapidly grew as an illustrator during the 1890s, and the in-demand artist was one of a long list of distinguished western painters who made outstanding pictorial contributions to western history and literature. He left behind about three thousand oils, watercolors, drawings and bronzes mainly on western subjects portraying archetypes of American life: the soldier, the cowboy, the rancher, the Indian, the horses and cattle of the plains. Remington left a remarkable historical record on canvas and in bronze. His bronze studies of American western lifestyles have universal appeal. "As long as there are such pictures and books as Remington's, Americans will remember the heritage of the frontier," wrote novelist Zane Grey.

Along with Charles M. Russell, the largely self-taught cowboy artist of Montana, these artist-illustrators of the American West broke away from European art traditions. Through painting the West and its peoples in an entirely realistic and authentic manner, they achieved one of America's major and still underappreciated contributions to the field of art.

The advent of western tourism coincided with and played a major role in the expansion of American cultural consciousness. The West of the expedition artists and illustrators was now accessible to cosmopolitan (and wealthy) easterners who eschewed Europe for the famed western United States. Arizona's exotic cultural attributes and climate did much to advance its popularity as a destination for tourists and artists alike.

Around the turn of the century, a new breed of painter started coming to Arizona—men of fine arts backgrounds, drawn by the inspiring play of light, clouds and dramatic landforms. The Santa Fe Railroad, often in exchange for paintings that were used to promote the booming Arizona tourism industry, brought many of them here. Promoters of the Santa Fe Railway sponsored artists to paint the Grand Canyon, seeking to commission academic, representational paintings that documented the Pueblo Indians of New Mexico and northern Arizona as well as the grandeur of the Grand Canyon, where the railway also owned and operated the El Tovar Hotel. The hotel even had an art gallery that carried works by many of the artists, an outlet for additional completed works. The painter received not only travel through the railroad but also, in many cases, room and board through the Santa Fe's concessionaire, the Fred Harvey Company. Year-round outdoor painting opportunities and the health benefits of temperate winters eventually attracted more than just a few artists.

In 1910, the Santa Fe Railroad invited a number of famous artists to participate in a journey along its line to the Grand Canyon. Among those who took the railroad up on this offer were Thomas Moran, Elliot Daingerfield, DeWitt Parshall, Edward Potthast and Frederick Ballard Williams. These artists spent ten days exploring the canyon, and the result, not surprisingly, was the creation of numerous magnificent Arizona landscape paintings.

In 1912, Arizona became a state. Its first governor, W.P. Hunt, quickly commissioned art depicting his state in the capitol building. Grand adventurer and western personality Lon Megargee was selected for the project of fifteen murals on the building hitting a cross-section of themes from Spanish colonial settlement, Indians and natural wonders to agriculture, mining and ranching. Megargee later gained extensive recognition for *The Cowboy's Dream*, a color print that featured a napping cowboy surrounded by cloud formations suggestive of scantily clad women.

The turn of the twentieth century was a critical time in the artistic identity of America. Artists fled Europe during World War I, and while many went back, they developed a taste for American culture. America's urban modernity—its towering skyscrapers and bridges, not to mention jazz—helped Americans carve an identity unique from Europe, still regarded as the world's center of culture.

Influenced by themes of technology, scientific knowledge and nostalgia, the painters of the early twentieth century found themselves intensely drawn to the new ground of the West. The call for an authentic and modern American art form became a national concern in the early decades of this new century. For many other artists of this period, it was the skyscraper and machines of mass production that became symbols of national identity and modernity. However, many artists feared that technology of the machine age would destroy the human spirit and so chose to explore the broad expanses and bold colors of the American landscape instead. These Anti-Modernists traveled west in search of an escape from the confines of modern life, hoping to create and define modern American art.

Arizona's roster of resident professional artists grew rapidly during these years though their backgrounds, media and reasons for coming to the state varied widely. Swedish-born Gunnar Widforss moved to the Grand Canyon in 1921 and painted hundreds of incredibly vibrant watercolors of the canyon and other parts of the area. Widforss had been educated as a muralist at Stockholm's Institute of Technology and was renowned as "the painter of the national parks." Widforss traveled extensively, but he became an American citizen in order to take up residency on the Grand Canyon's rim. In fact, he died and was buried there in 1934.

But the most well-known modern artist dedicated to portraying the state's essence may well be Lafayette Maynard Dixon. A California native, Dixon worked as a cowboy and roamed throughout the Southwest, spending considerable time in Arizona, but he had also worked in New York and San Francisco as an accomplished illustrator for newspapers and magazines. Turning to easel painting, he found his true calling. By 1928, Maynard Dixon had established himself as a first-rate ethnographic artist. His work was influenced by some aspects of the Cubist movement and developed a very strong design element. Typically, his subjects were western landscapes and their native peoples. He was at this time commissioned to design ingenious subject tapestries for the Arizona Biltmore in Phoenix planned by architect Frank Lloyd Wright. Dixon ended his days in 1946 in Tucson.

With the exception of a very few artists whose work remained in demand with tourists throughout the Depression, most Arizona art professionals joined the ranks of participants in the Federal Art Project (FAP) begun in 1933. The last of these programs ran until 1943, ultimately providing employment for around sixty artists in Arizona. Many of the works (murals, sculptures, paintings) produced within this public arts endeavor remain in Arizona and can still be viewed in and around public buildings and institutions depicting mainly historical subject matter.

During the Depression years, several local artists gained substantial recognition for their efforts. Arizona native and modernist Lew Davis received his formal art education from the National Academy of Design in New York and then returned to his hometown of Jerome for a five-year project known as the Jerome Series. These paintings and prints were conceived in a manner similar to the Mexican muralists of the time and were expressive of the people, activities and atmosphere of this quintessential Arizona mining community.

Among the other notable artists who have visited and worked in Arizona are Adolph Gottlieb, an initial participant in the Abstract Expressionist movement; Max Ernst, the quintessential Surrealist; and David Hockney, a central figure in the modern art world. Gottlieb resigned from the Federal Art Project in 1937, and his wife, Esther, came to Arizona seeking temporary artistic respite from the New York art scene of the late 1930s. They moved to an adobe house outside Tucson. They intended to stay one year but became subtly inspired by the rock art in the Southwest.

Max Ernst's visitation of Arizona was even more artistically monumental than Gottlieb's. He and his wife, Dorothea Tanning, took solace in the desert's isolation. For Ernst, this proved to be a very crucial period, as it was here that he sculpted in concrete his most important sculpture, *Capricorn*. The cheapness of available concrete was the area's greatest asset to Ernst. In addition, Sedona's landscape almost duplicated the artist's rugged fantasies and dreams, differing only in the deep red color of the rocks, which later became the subject of *Colline Inspiree*, called his finest painting of Arizona.

With the rise of Abstract Expressionism in the 1940s to 1950s, America became fully independent of European artistic traditions and established its preeminent position as leader in the contemporary visual arts. Ernst would have a huge influence on another giant of the art world: Jackson Pollock. Pollock has become the artist who, as his rival and colleague Willem de Kooning said, broke the ice of what is now called Abstract Expressionism by his signature drips, splatters and overlays of lacy lines and paint puddles, which merge into an abstract expression of self. This breakthrough shifted the center of the art world from Europe to the United States, specifically New York, at midcentury. Pollock's flat canvasses were the signal development of the age and the next phase after the innovations of Pablo Picasso. Abstract Expressionism gives primacy to individual expression. In popular culture of the time, Pollock's art was a lightning rod for asking the age-old question of what defines art.

Most people are not aware that Pollock's artistic roots lay in the western American landscape, not New York. All swagger and cowboy boots, he cultivated a western identity not only in his art but also in his persona. Pollock experimented with painting western subjects early in his career, specifically in *Going West* (1934–35). *Going West* depicts the migration of farmers going to California and is the piece that gave influential artists, friends and family members the extra confidence to support Pollock's ambitions. The struggling Pollock family moved from place to place, including the Salt River Valley in Arizona, where Pollock's father turned the sandy soil into a dairy farm using irrigation canals modeled on those of the ancient Hohokam culture. During several summers, Pollock worked on survey crews, including a memorable one in 1927, when, at age fifteen, he worked on one crew on the north rim of the Grand Canyon. In Arizona, Pollock also discovered American Indian art and culture, which would become a lifelong interest. Pollock would become a foundational figure in modern art.

Hardly a movement or epoch of art history has run its course—Plein-Air, art of the American West, Surrealism, Abstract Expressionism—that could not find one of its aficionados traveling or working within the state of Arizona. Works resulting from Arizona's landscape and artists' experiences and interactions with its culture make up a unique microcosm of American art, and the state will undoubtedly continue to be a dynamic place for many contemporary mediums.

3

THE VERDE VALLEY

"I don't have a window because I don't want realism to foul up my art."
—Max Ernst

When English writer J.B. Priestly traveled to Arizona and recorded his reactions to the varied environment of the Mogollon Rim and the Grand Canyon, he wrote, "Oak Creek is Arizona turned idyllic. Here the mountains have married the desert…If you filmed the extravagant place you would be accused of impudent and careless faking. I felt like saying that at last we had arrived in Avalon and must stay here forever, vanishing from the world that has known us. Why go on?"

Located between the present towns of Flagstaff and Prescott, Arizona's Verde Valley, a land of basins, ranges and plateaus, is one of the loveliest valleys in the state, a place that has impressed many a creator. From the ancient Singagua tribe leaving enigmatic petroglyphs or "rock art" on the canyon walls around Oak Creek to today's photographers, painters, sculptors and mixed-media artists, the Verde Valley—and particularly the town of Sedona—has been a melting pot for creativity.

Dripping with history, the first Anglo-American settlers in the valley migrated here in search of a richer life in the territory that would become Arizona. Pioneers crossed great distances to stake out farms in the Verde; those who settled found a new beginning in this oasis of cottonwood trees and streams. Many of the pioneers settled along Oak Creek, where they found an abundance of good water and land that would support anything from cabbages to roses and fish to Hereford cattle. Over time, populations increased, and villages grew.

A pioneer in both the Dada and Surrealist movements, German artist Max Ernst and his wife, Dorothea Tanning, moved to Sedona in 1946. Ernst, the protégé of Salvadore Dalí and Pablo Picasso, claimed that there are only two places in the world that he would like to live—Paris or Sedona. In 1943, the town had few people and consisted of little more than a gas station, post office, general store and bar. According to friends, it was the sort of solitude Ernst needed.

The Surrealist movement was founded in 1924 in Paris by poet André Breton, but its origins can be traced to the French poets Baudelaire and Rimbaud and Italian painter Giorgio de Chirico. As an art form, Surrealism generated shock and surprise through the unexpected juxtapositions of objects or ideas. In the 1930s, many Surrealist artists immigrated to the United States on the eve of World War II, and new aesthetics celebrating dreams, irrationalism, fantasy and absurdity released new interpretations of the West. For many people, including Ernst, Arizona was surreal to its core, a place of constant opposites and contradictions. He was continually experimenting with mediums to develop unique approaches. Although Ernst was not the first artist to utilize concrete for sculpture, the concept of applying concrete reliefs to cinder blocks to be incorporated into his Sedona home was out of the ordinary. Ernst's career during the 1940s and early 1950s was not financially successful; thus, concrete presented itself as an inexpensive medium. Sedona was the location for the creation of perhaps his best-known sculpture, *Capricorn*, begun in 1948 and finally cast into bronze in 1962 in France

Though famed anthropologist Claude Lévi-Strauss considered Max Ernst the most important artist of the twentieth century, Ernst is certainly one of the least well known. The fact that the majority of his works are in private hands is a contributing factor, but there are others.

Born in the German town of Bruhl, in 1909, Ernst enrolled at the University of Bonn, planning to study philosophy and psychiatry. However, he had already started painting silly variations on the prevailing styles of Cubism and Futurism, and soon, he abandoned his studies for painting entirely. Other eccentric visionaries gave voice to the general disorientation of the day—artists, poets, musicians and moviemakers expressed themselves in mystifying but exciting new artistic forms. "Seeing was my chief preoccupation. My eyes were greedy not only for the amazing world which assaulted them from without but also for that other mysterious disturbing world which surged up and melted away in my dreams," said a young Ernst.

DADA

Then came World War I. Ernst was drafted and spent four years as an artillery engineer. When the war ended, he went to Cologne, pausing only to marry Luise Strauss, his university girlfriend. Ernst's work had been undergoing a transformation. While holed up in a hotel room in a Rhineland town, he had become enthralled by a catalogue containing advertisements showing objects related to anthropology, mineralogy and paleontology. In 1913, his works were shown in Berlin alongside those of Paul Klee, Marc Chagall and Hans Arp. After being nearly court-martialed for insubordination during military service in the war, Ernst was ripe for joining Dada, the art movement that arose in New York and Zurich around 1916.

Outraged at the savagery of war, referring to the bloodbath as "the dirtiest of tricks," Ernst and fellow artists like Arp and Marcel Duchamp turned against all forms of reason, authority and convention. As the Continent emerged from World War I, European art craved spontaneity and irrationality. Americans remember the 1920s as a lighthearted and prosperous era, but in Europe, the people were disheartened by the way in which war had disrupted the society they had always known.

Max Ernst and Dorothea Tanning stand in front of his studio with Wilson Mountain in the background. *Courtesy of the Sedona Historical Society.*

The leading agitators in the movement called themselves Dadaists. "Contrary to general belief, dada did not want to shock the bourgeois. They were already shocked enough. No, dada was a rebellious upsurge of vital energy and rage; it resulted from the absurdity, the whole immense piggishness of that imbecilic war," said Ernst. At the same time the artist was experimenting with other methods of collage, juxtaposing fragments of newspaper advertisements and photographs. But where the Cubists had been striving for a logical, visually harmonious whole, Ernst and his fellows reveled in all combinations of totally unrelated images and the resulting social, political and erotic implications. His Dada collages and photomontages included *Here Everything Is Still Floating* (1920), a shockingly illogical composition made from cutout photographs of insects, fish and anatomical drawings arranged to suggest the multiple identity of the things depicted.

In 1920, Ernst exhibited his revolutionary collages in Paris and moved to the French capital as a leading proponent of Surrealism in painting. His work has been described as meditative, ingenious, explorative, humorous and anticipating Dalí and is known for bizarre imagery; he consistently uses the known to evoke the unknown. In his nontraditional paintings, collages and photomontages, his art embodied invention, discovery and revelation.

THE BIRTH OF SURREALISM

In 1922, Ernst left his wife; his infant son, Jimmy; and a job at his father-in-law's hat machinery factory to go to Paris, perhaps influenced by poet Andre Breton's (a co-founder of the Surrealist movement) influential article titled "Lachez Tout" ("Drop Everything") in which Breton advised his colleagues to quit their jobs, their daily routines—even their families—and head out. Travel would offer a fresh start and maybe even a cure for the ills and ennui inflicted by World War I.

Composed entirely of fractious leaders, the Dada movement self-destructed in 1924, but Ernst's work already heralded the next major art movement: Surrealism, which places more emphasis on improvisation than Dada art did. Its practitioners hoped to create a spontaneous art that would draw solely on the unconscious establishing a super-reality that was superior to the mundane world of logic. Again Ernst was in the forefront; he became a founding member of the Surrealists, a group of artists and writers whose work grew out of fantasies evoked from the unconscious. Ernst had always relied heavily on dream imagery.

Though Marcel Duchamp, the French Dadaist, and Salvador Dalí, the Spanish Surrealist, may be individually more widely known, Ernst is the only artist whose career spans both movements. To stimulate the flow of imagery from his unconscious mind, Ernst began in 1925 to use the techniques of frottage (pencil rubbings of such things as wood grain, fabric or leaves) and decalcomania. He allowed free association to suggest images he subsequently used in a series of drawings ("Histoire Naturelle," 1926) and in many paintings, such as *The Great Forest* (1927) and *The Temptation of St. Anthony* (1945). These vast landscapes stem ultimately from the tradition of nature mysticism of the German Romantics. Ernst's *Two Children Threatened by a Nightingale* is the ultimate Surrealist work. It is said to have originated from a hallucination the artist experienced when he was ill as a young child.

In the 1930s, with Hitler in power, Ernst reflected his feelings in a series of canvases he titled "The Entire City." After 1934, Ernst's activities centered increasingly on sculpture, for which he used improvised techniques, just as he had in painting.

THE WAR YEARS

Persecuted in France for being German and by Germans for being anti-Nazi, Ernst was forced to leave Europe during World War II, not without having spent a bit of time at a French prison camp. Even there, he kept on painting. When friends won parole for him, he fled to Marseilles, where thousands were seeking permits to evacuate. Fortunately, he met Peggy Guggenheim, the American copper heiress and art collector who, before the war, had already started amassing an impressive collection of twentieth-century art from Paris and London. With Peggy's assistance, in July 1941, he, Peggy and her two children flew to America. Ernst married Peggy the following year. They set up house in a brownstone on Manhattan's Beekman Place. Other artists and Surrealists had also fled to New York, including Breton, Fernand Leger, Marc Chagall and Piet Mondian. Younger American artists avidly studied the exhibitions of these exiles in Manhattan galleries, including Peggy Guggenheim's the Art of this Century gallery.

Beekman Place became a hive of parties, with a guest list ranging from Clifford Odets to Gypsy Rose Lee. Ernst, however, was (as usual) caught up in experiment, this time, with something called "oscillation." It involved punching a hole in the bottom of a tin can, filling the can with paint and then swinging it by a string over a canvas. The result was thin, ropy crisscrossed lines that looked surprisingly like the drip paintings a young American named Jackson Pollock would make famous only a few years later.

IN SEDONA

In 1943, Ernst met a young American Surrealist painter, Dorothea Tanning. Ernst divorced Peggy Guggenheim and married Dorothea in 1946. As Ernst and his wife were traveling by car all the way from New York to California, they crossed the Sedona desert, and Max was fascinated to find that what he had painted in his works was alive there, away from all the madding crowds. There were no resorts in Sedona at the time and no homes available in the area, but Max decided that he had to build a house right there, by the side of the landscapes that had inspired him before he even knew they existed. Dorothea owned land near Black's ranch in what is now a heavily populated area of Sedona.

Tanning began drawing as a child while living with her family in Galesburg, Illinois. Discouraged from pursuing an art career early in life, she began working at the public library, where she read works by Oscar Wilde, Edgar Allen Poe and Gustave Flaubert. These authors were perhaps the major influence on her becoming a Surrealist artist, since this movement was primarily literary in its beginnings. Tanning's art matured during the 1940s, when she concurrently painted, designed scenery and costumes and even participated in Hans Richter's film *Dreams That Money Can Buy* (1945).

Tanning, in her autobiography *Birthday*, wrote of the couple's time in Sedona:

> And these are incomparable years. We build the house—of wood, for there is no water; we chase away the cattle from our five tomato plants; we haul ice twenty miles from Cottonwood... The place is not a town nor yet a village. A general store dispenses beer and cattle feed and there are lovelorn tunes in the jukebox ("That Old Black Magic"). Hear the twangy jokes of cowhands. "Hi, Max!" they say, sizing us up, taking us in, giving us the benefit of the doubt. "You paint scenes?" Down the road is the post

office, exactly eight by eight, Coke dispenser outside. Miraculously letters sometimes arrive.

Though the Sedona days were days of poverty for Ernst and Dorothea, Ernst always turned the houses in which he lived into works of art, and the Sedona, Arizona home was no exception. The home Ernst built was unique in design but lacked the architectural perfection a contractor could have provided. Its most outstanding feature was a hallway with an altitude of seventeen feet built to accommodate some wooden statues carved by Indians in British Columbia. Max made huge sculptures that adorned the yard, and he enjoyed one of the most productive periods in his life as an artist. While Ernst feared the realism a window would bring to his art, he also feared the change in color perception it would bring. The dominant color in Sedona is red. "If anything bothered him about Sedona, it was the red rock," said Nassan Gobran. "Max saw red rock in all his work. If he looked out the window while he painted he could not tell if the blue on the canvas was purple because of all the red he saw."

In the six years that marked his Sedona period, Ernst was a prolific painter, though his time in Arizona was predominantly occupied with sculptural work. Noteworthy among his output was *Spring in Paris, Inspired Hillock*, a painting that, despite its title, contains many silhouettes and colors of the rimrock country. He exercised his abilities as a sculptor by producing a monumental cement piece entitled *Capricorn*. Interestingly, early Dada fantasies by Ernst depicted bizarre, barren, rocky landscapes, and upon visiting the Sedona area, he must certainly have felt he had discovered a landscape of his dreams. *Colline Inspiree* (1950) and *Arizona Landscape* (1959) show his interaction with the flaming red aspects of the Sedona rocks under certain climatic conditions and the bizarre rock formations found in the countryside.

In 1949, Dylan Thomas was passing through Sedona and ended up staying with Ernst for over a month. Thomas read his poetry at several places in a dull monotone, and everyone enjoyed it, even if not everyone understood it. While in Arizona, Ernst befriended the state's most important artists, Frederick Sommer and Lew Davis.

Nassan Gobran recalls the day he left: "I ran into him at the Shell station where he was putting gas in his car. The back of his station wagon was full of paintings and he was looking around at the mountains. 'Why couldn't I have been born a grocer or something?' he said. 'Then I wouldn't have to leave Sedona.'"

Jimmy Ernst and Nassan Gobran with Max Ernst sculpture *Capricorn. Courtesy of the Sedona Historical Society.*

Tanning's *Autoportrait* of 1944 appears nostalgic for a place she remembered and a place to which she desired to return: the red sandstone cliffs of the Sedona region. Sadly, Ernst and Tanning's house in Sedona has been remodeled beyond recognition by its current owner.

In 1949, upon a return to France, where Ernst was becoming something of a national celebrity, his work became less experimental; he spent much time perfecting his modeling technique in traditional sculptural materials, and he reclaimed some of the elements that had characterized his production in the 1920s. In 1963, the couple established themselves on a hilltop in Seillans in a modern village designed by Dorothea and decorated with Max's art. There he developed a new etching technique.

Still, he was never content with any of his many innovations, saying, "A painter is lost if he finds himself."

Little is left of Ernst in Sedona to remind people he spent six years of his life here. Most of Ernst's statues, dreamed up off and on for thirty years, stand in private gardens in France and Switzerland, with one, *Lunar Asparagus*, housed in the Museum of Modern Art in New York City. Probably of all Ernst's work, the dark miasmic dream forests he was painting when he fled to the United States at the outset of World War II are those with which Americans are most familiar. In the extraordinary range of his styles and techniques, Ernst is to Dada and Surrealism what Picasso is to twentieth-century art as a whole; his life exemplifies those aspects of the countervailing movements of twentieth-century art, in which the mysterious and irrational predominated.

THE FOUNDING OF AN ARTS CENTER

Egyptian sculptor Nassan Gobran previously taught in Boston and had been invited to Oak Creek Canyon to consider a teaching position. Before coming to Arizona, Gobran's work was exhibited in London, Paris, New York, Boston, many New England museums and Cairo, Egypt. Since living in Arizona, he has had one-man shows at the Phoenix Art Museum and Yares Gallery while exhibiting frequently at the Sedona Arts Center.

Born in Egypt, Gobran earned an MFA from the Royal Academy of Art at Cairo University. From 1939 to 1946, he headed the sculpture department of the Fine Arts School in Cairo and executed monumental sculptures for the royal family. He came to the Boston Museum of Fine Arts on a fellowship as the result of his work in Cairo. In 1948, he was appointed to head the Berkshire Festival and Music Center's scenic department and to designs sets for the opera *The Turk* in Italy. This experience, he later said, was very much an influence on his later dream of establishing a cultural center in Sedona.

In 1950, Nassan first came to Sedona as the founder and director of the Art Department of Verde Valley School, where he remained for three years. After seeing the movie *Broken Arrow*, which was shot in the vicinity of Oak Creek, Gobran decided he was meant to move west, decreeing that such an exquisite setting needed an official place for artists to gather and create. When he left the school in 1953, he rented the studio of the

Nassan Gobran puts the finishing touches on a sculpture for the Sedona Arts Center. *Courtesy of Sedona Historical Society.*

world-famous artist Max Ernst while Ernst and his wife, Dorothea, were in Paris. In this studio on Brewer Road, Nassan spent the next seven years absorbed in his sculpture and architectural designing. From the moment Gobran arrived in Sedona, he was overwhelmed by the magnificent scenery and came to feel that the place was ideally adapted for the sort of center he had in mind.

Gobran worked tirelessly for his dream of an art center. As Sedona continued to inspire all who settled in its high desert realm of beauty into the next decade, Gobran and a group of local visionaries—including George Babbitt Jr.; his wife, Madeline Hunter Babbitt; Nick Duncan; Bill and Helen Frye; and Cecil Lockhart-Smith—acknowledged the need for a place where the town's artists could work, teach and collaborate. In

Susan Kliewer. *Sedona*. Bronze. *Courtesy of Sedona Chamber of Commerce & Tourism Bureau.*

At the opening of the Sedona Arts Center, Nassan Gobran, the founding president, models a head in clay. *Courtesy of Sedona Historical Society.*

1958, they established Sedona's first arts center, originally called "Canyon Kiva." They purchased the historic Jordan Apple Packing Barn, which had been previously used for apples and peaches, and it quickly became the community's informal creative and social hub as simply the Art Barn. The Sedona Arts Center became a reality with Nassan as its founding president. This groundbreaking project soon influenced many other communities around the state, from Yuma to Flagstaff, to start their own art centers.

During the early 1960s, Sedona was rich with artists, entrepreneurs and city refugees who foresaw the area's potential and contributed to its explosive development. Through all the growth and demographic changes, the arts center remained one of the cultural constants in town.

Lee Blackwell. *Arc Fountain*. Copper. *Courtesy of Sedona Chamber of Commerce & Tourism Bureau.*

Nassan Gobran. *Peace.* Concrete. 1982. *Courtesy of Sedona Chamber of Commerce & Tourism Bureau.*

A community theater was founded there in 1970. By 2001, the mission of the center was redefined to focus primarily on education through the School of the Arts and gallery exhibitions of its visual arts. The School of the Arts continues to catalyze the creative development of students of all ages and backgrounds.

COWBOY ARTISTS OF AMERICA

In addition to an arts center, a highly significant organization would have its beginning in the town—the Cowboy Artists of America (CAA). Over the years, the Cowboy Artists of America have become something of a legend. They began as renegades who bucked the establishment in order to promote a style and subject outside the mainstream.

"Cowboy art" is a specific term that is part of a genre known as art of the American West. In 1965, the birth of the organization grew out of a meeting of cowboy artists George Phippen, Charlie Dye, Joe Beeler and John Hampton in Sedona at Oak Creek Tavern. By this year, these were four accomplished artists with successful careers and established individual reputations and their own audiences for contemporary western art. In Sedona, on a hot Arizona afternoon, the four of them talked, laughed, drank and founded the organization of artists that would become a full-blown cultural phenomenon.

A few days later, in Dye's Sedona studio, the four met again to formalize their ideas for the new organization. They agreed on the name of the organization, Cowboy Artists of America, and fleshed out their objectives. According to its founding document, the organization exists "to perpetuate the memory and culture of the Old West as typified by the late Frederic Remington, Charles Russell, and others; to insure [*sic*] authentic representations of the life of the West, as it was and is; to maintain standards of quality in contemporary Western painting, drawing and sculpture; [and] to help guide collectors of Western art."

Like the Impressionists, who challenged an undeviating academic style with painterly brushwork, the cowboy artists rejuvenated representational art during an era dominated by abstraction. Cowboy art was in and of itself a form of anti-modernism in which the romance of the West as an untamed land of cowboys and Indians still existed. The genre could trace its roots to the early statehood days. One of Arizona's early cowboy artists was Ross Santee, who took up work on a ranch along the Gila River in 1915. Santee provided countless marvelously effective nostalgic sketches of Southwestern ranching and Native American scenes that decorated the publication *Arizona Highways* for years to come.

During the 1960s, the cowboy artists joined forces, specifically to market their western realism when most gallery walls were filled with East Coast minimalism. CAA not only helped erode the grip that abstract art held over the contemporary arts community of the 1960s onward, but it also significantly contributed to a growing respect for regional art during the 1970s and 1980s. Indeed, more than any other group of artists, the cowboy artists have called national and international attention to the fine arts of the American West. Their spectacular success has defied the notion that New York is the only place to find great art, and moreover, they have demonstrated that some of the best-quality art is being created west of the Mississippi River. In recalling the group's modest beginnings, Beeler has commented, "We had

Left to right: Joe Beeler, Charlie Dye, John Hampton and George Phippen meet up at a Cowboy Artists of America organizational meeting at Bird's Bar. *Courtesy of Sedona Historical Society.*

no idea how successful Cowboy Artists of America would be. Today though, I think art historians would say that the impact of the association has gone far beyond the bounds of Western or Cowboy Art. It's been a big boost for realism in all American art, no matter what the theme."

The first president of the Cowboy Artists of America was Prescott's own George Phippen, a western artist extraordinaire. Born in 1915, Phippen was raised on farms in Iowa and Kansas and had no formal art education. While serving in World War II, he taught himself to paint, and soon after the war, he briefly worked in Santa Fe, New Mexico. As he began to work in oil and watercolor, art became his life. In Prescott, he opened his first official

Clyde Ross Morgan. *Red Rocks and the Cowboy Artist*. Bronze. 2002. *Courtesy of Sedona Chamber of Commerce & Tourism Bureau.*

studio, rapidly establishing his reputation as a western artist researching the background, elements, people and settings to portray his subjects with as much authentic detail as possible. Although George had a brief career of only twenty years, he produced around three thousand works and is best remembered for his bronze sculptures, including pieces like *Cowboy in a Storm*.

Word spread quickly of the new upstart organization, and informal applications for membership began to come in from all over the West and even the East. Cowboy artist Bill Nebeker describes with romantic imagery the organization's most important event: the annual trail ride of the artists—or, as he calls it, "the glue that keeps the group close and encouraging." On the ride, members go on horseback to round up cattle over high mountains; through hot, cactus-filled deserts; across the vast open plains of Nebraska; along the California coastal grasslands; and even down from the high volcanic ranges of the Parker Ranch in Hawaii, the largest ranch in America. Personal conversations during the event build deep, abiding and lifelong friendships that keep the Cowboy Artists of America so very unique and the basis of the organization. "These friendships become real when we all get away from the museums, galleries, collectors and even our wives and kids on the trail rides each year," said Nebeker. "As the artists get out into the open spaces and visit different cattle ranches all over the country, meeting and spending time with real working cowboys, the ranch owners and families who still truly live the life of the West become like family." Whatever the source of the magic, the CAA has the distinction of being the longest-running organization of artists of any genre and is credited with being the single most influential factor in popularizing western art during the second half of the twentieth century.

JEROME

OFF THE RADAR ARTISTS MECCA

Leaving Sedona, one passes through rather unremarkable Verde Valley towns that resemble any other towns in Arizona. Then there is remarkable Jerome, perched high above and quite unlike any place most of us have been.

Jerome rests against Cleopatra Hill, a mountain once rich in copper, gold and silver. After miners staked their claims here in the 1870s, there was nowhere to go but rich. By 1929, Jerome had boomed to become Arizona's third-largest town with some 2,400 miners working vast, open pits and eighty-eight miles of dark shafts and tunnels. In 1953, mining stopped, and many people left the shaky town. Jerome has come back to economic life as the refuge of many artists and writers, the "heart of the town's quirky, and sometimes contentious, soulfulness," remarks Diane Rapaport, a distinguished and personable local author.

Though a mere hour from Sedona, today, Jerome is nationally recognized as an art mecca in its own right, although exactly why is cause for debate. Though the town shares many similarities with Sedona and other arts towns, such as Taos and San Miguel de Allende, Mexico, exactly why such a high percentage of the creative sorts reside here is hard to pinpoint. The town's aesthetics draw artists to it like bees to honey; few other art towns command the spectacular 180-mile panorama view that Jerome has from its steep mountain perch.

Though the town's status as an artist mecca is a recent phenomenon, there were earlier artists drawn here for many of the same motives. "When I rounded a hairpin curve on the no guardrail road over the mountain from Prescott to Jerome, and saw Jerome with Clarkdale and the Verde Valley stretched out below, I drew a deep breath and thought 'this is it.'"—thus began Henry H. Strater's six-year experience in the Southwest, away from his native New England. Strater brought with him a broad experience of the study of painting and sculpture at the Academie Julien in Paris, the Art Students League in New York, the Pennsylvania Academy of Fine Arts in Philadelphia and the Maurice Denis School. His early admiration of the art of Paul Cézanne is prevalent in many of his Arizona works, including *Storm along the Verde* (1937). Strater recalls this canvas was painted around Christmas time from the hill on which the nearby Rimrock Ranch stood.

When big mining abandoned Jerome in 1953, the first artists moved in and organized to support one another and draw attention to Jerome art. Roger Holt, who had exhibited at the Metropolitan Museum of Art, Corcoran Gallery and Carnegie Institute, moved to Jerome in 1954 and lived there until the mid-1960s. His wife, Shan Holt, founded a group called the Verde Valley Artists. Shan found a patron and friend in portrait artist Lilli Brant, who became president of the group. Interestingly, as the town struggled to survive, Lilli's husband, the renowned geophysicist Arthur Brant, predicted that someday Jerome would become an art destination.

In 1975, the Verde Valley Artist group morphed into a formal nonprofit called the Verde Valley Artists Association (VVAA), which started featuring non-Jerome artists for major Jerome exhibitions. One featured Paolo Soleri, the Italian architect who built the futuristic desert city Arcosanti, and another show featured Lew Davis, an eminent Arizona artist who grew up in Jerome during its mining days. The VVAA began a student art show that toured the state and sponsored studio tours. Many artists report that they sold their first pieces of art to people attending those tours. These activities garnered support from many Verde Valley businesses and helped place Jerome on the map as an art destination. From 1953 onward, the community of Jerome actively supported its artists. The Jerome Historical Society donated space to the Verde Valley Artists Association and rented space to other artists at very low costs. It also voted to dedicate some of its budget to buy art, as did the town of Jerome. Both the society and the town boast extensive and valuable art collections, as do many of its residents and businesses.

Since the 1970s, the town's unusually high ratio of artists to residents—almost half of the four hundred or so of its permanent residents are artists—have brought much character and pizzazz to the town. Many artists own successful shops and galleries. The oldest of the Uptown galleries is Made in Jerome, co-founded in 1972 by potter David Hall and two students from nearby Prescott College. A brief stroll around the town allows you to pass by other artist-owned galleries and shops in the main part of town, including Nellie Bly II, owned by painter Diane Geoghegan; Aurum Jewelry, co-owned by artist Sharon Watson; Raku Gallery, owned by glass blower and potter Tracy Weisel; and Designs on You, owned by Leigh Hay Martin, a gifted quilter. Artists own and operate all the studio businesses in the high school complex: "The Old Jerome High School is filled with artist studios and great artistic energy...it is a very fluid group that constantly has new people in the spaces," says Donna Chesler, owner of Gallery 527. Chesler adores the Wild West spirit of Jerome that is entrenched in its residents. "Jerome has attracted a wonderful group of free spirits. Famous people can stay under the radar, and emerging artists will be lovingly encouraged to grow."

What does, in the end, distinguish Jerome is perhaps the fact that many Jerome artists participate in local politics. The prevailing philosophy here among this group is that people who do not protect their own liberty can simply lose it. Artists quickly learned that if they wanted a say in the safety, restoration and future of the town, they needed to actively involve themselves. This spurred involvement in drafting Jerome's Comprehensive Plan and Zoning and Design Review ordinances.

Artists have been elected to many local governmental departments, such as the Jerome Town Council, and have been appointed to serve on the Planning and Zoning and Design Review, as well as having served on the Jerome Fire Department and fire auxiliary. Their contributions and business endeavors help counter the oft-spoken opinions that the hippies who moved to Jerome were spaced-out, stoned good-for-nothings and that artists dare not meddle in politics or attempt to become successful business owners.

After more than sixty years of restoration, the ghost town derelict that Jerome had become is gone; it is arguably one of the most photographed and painted towns in America. The town's twenty-five galleries and studios are held together by the Jerome Art Walk group. "This gives lots of space for artists to show their work. Many of us are proud to be galleries that show only local work. The Jerome Artist's Co-op is a perfect example of this," says Chesler. Among this nurturing group, local means the whole Verde Valley region and not just Jerome.

Among Jerome's artists, many are notable indeed. Paul Nonnast was one of four runner-ups in the Washington, D.C. Vietnam War Memorial design competition for his stainless steel obelisk mounted on a floating disk that swayed in the wind. Nonnast lived in a hand-built stone house with rocks collected from the hills surrounding Jerome. A painter, sculptor, toolmaker, architect, stonemason and graphic designer, Nonnast was one of the "few artists whose emotional style and meticulous finish defined every piece of work that he undertook, all demonstrating a highly evolved aesthetic," shares Rapaport. "No artist in Jerome came close to his level of excellence and originality and style. You could hand me a piece of his work that I had never seen, in any media, and I'd be able to identify the artist as Paul."

Artists continue to be attracted to the Verde Valley for its cultural attributes, artistic legacy and geographical beauty, as well as the professional opportunities available through the Sedona Arts Center and its many world-renowned festivals. Jerome will most likely remain an art destination with its heavy tourist numbers on par with Sedona.

Today, many Jerome and Sedona residents create world-class art in virtually every media and show in dozens of galleries, shops and art studios. "As an arts mecca, Jerome resident artists are deeply entwined in the collective identity of the town and find themselves bumping into each other along its tiny side streets," observes Rapaport. "Perhaps in the end it is the peaceful isolation and knowing that at night there is nothing to do than your art and gazing at the stars."

4
PORTRAITS OF THE ARTISTS

MAXFIELD PARRISH

There is in it at times a wild fiendish delight which partakes of all sorts of sensations of what is possible in art and in me and in everything.

The famous artist and illustrator Maxfield Parrish first visited Arizona as a young man, and the state's dramatic sunsets, rugged canyons and rock art helped to inspire his palette and technique. Parrish lived and painted in Sedona in 1901–02, a brief but significant time period. In 1901, he completed a series of illustrations of Arizona that brought him instant fame and success. The influence of the red rocks is especially apparent in his later art. Known as the common man's Rembrandt, in a hurrying world where skies were too often gray, his trademarks were lush gardens, ecstatic women and his celebrated "Parrish blue."

He completed enchanting children's book illustrations and magazine covers, ambitious murals and lonely landscapes. When he died in 1966 at age ninety-five, Parrish was in again. Critics called him a precursor of pop art; Andy Warhol collected his work. College students in the 1960s recall hanging Maxfield Parrish in dorms once again.

A generation after his death, Maxfield Parrish remains one of America's best- and least-known artists. At the height of his career, a Parrish print hung in one out of every four American homes. Though his utopias still adorn calendars and posters, few people have ever seen his paintings in person. His career belies many a myth about the temperamental artist. The story of his life contains no anguished searching, no struggle for acceptance.

Gifted from childhood, he earned commissions even before finishing art school. Throughout his career and until trembling hands forced him to stop painting, he never lacked a market. The Parrishes were an old Philadelphia Quaker family. As a boy, Parrish drew dragons and then cut and pasted them into pictures. As an adult, he spent as much time as he could in his machine shop, building intricate models of the houses, barns, castles and pillars that he captured in his paintings. Parrish often belittled himself as "a businessman with a brush."

In 1888, Parrish entered Pennsylvania's Haverford College intending to study architecture. At the Pennsylvania Academy of Fine Arts (PAFA), he was hailed as "one of the most brilliant and most suggestive decorative painters in the country." After executing his first commission—wall paintings for the University of Pennsylvania's Mask and Wig Club—Parrish's designs for the project were soon displayed in New York, where a Harper's editor asked Parrish to do a cover. The 1895 Easter issue of *Harper's Bazaar* introduced the nation to the man who would dominate the art of illustration in its golden age.

The great outdoors were a passion, fascination and devotion so strong for Parrish that in the last phase of his career, he painted nothing but landscapes. Of his days at Haverford, he wrote, "Lying under those copper beeches, when we should have been doing something else, looking into the cathedral windows above did a lot more for us than contemplation of the Roman Coliseum. There were grand trees in those days and grand trees do something to you."

AMERICA'S GOLDEN AGE OF ILLUSTRATION

The time was ripe for the zenith of American illustrative art, promulgated by Howard Pyle and marked by the work of N.C. Wyeth, Frank Schoonover, Violet Oakley, Jessie Willcox Smith, Elizabeth Shippen Green—and Maxfield Parrish. From the 1870s to the 1910s, as magazines blossomed on newsstands, many whose paintings would later hang in museums began their careers as illustrators.

The turn of the twentieth century was far from the quaint and relatively slow-moving time present-day Americans might imagine. Starting in 1890, the decade during which Parrish began to make his first impressions as a painter and illustrator, the United States was still taming its wild frontiers while also rushing helter-skelter to build modern culture. The last of the territories appropriated from Native American nations were still being opened up for settlers as Thomas Edison was given a patent for the first U.S. motion picture camera. The automobile was a big gadget still being tinkered with in experimenters' sheds, airplanes were an oncoming dream, radio transmission was an enticing idea yet to be realized and the telephone had only just begun appearing in American households. The mass media of the time were all print: newspapers, a growing number of magazines and books of all sizes and subject matters.

Winslow Homer drew for *Harper's Weekly*. Books and magazines were the primary source of entertainment and information in this era. Stories—from ancient Arthurian legends to new American fables like the *Wonderful Wizard of Oz*—were avidly read by a highly literate population eager for new tales. At the same time, improvements in printing technology made it possible for color illustrations to appear with the stories, supplementing the words more vividly than before.

That this new technology was a hugely liberating element for artists and publishers and a bonus and delight for readers is amply evidenced by the surge in colorfully illustrated books and magazines that occurred during the golden age of illustration. Readers testify to being swept more deeply into a story by its vibrant images. Under the watchful eyes of talented and dedicated publishing house art directors, the colorful stories within stories by the artists of the golden age were reproduced in books and magazines as faithfully as technology allowed, bringing the art of illustration at its very best into tens of millions of homes.

Parrish's ability to put himself in the child's place, to peer into a story and see its characters—how the light played over their faces, how dragons might converse quite rationally—made him the perfect collaborator for authors whose books were aimed at young and adventurous spirits. Interestingly, when placed beside the body of other works he produced—landscape paintings, calendars, posters, magazine covers—his illustrations for books are relatively few.

And young people were the primary beneficiaries of this artistry. A number of magazines—including *Harper's Young People*—as well as many of the most lavishly illustrated books published during the golden age were created to appeal to the young or at the young at heart. It was in illustrating such broadly appealing stories that many of the illustrators of America's golden age found their most memorable subjects and acquired legions of rapt admirers. The talent, discipline and vision of these artists tied to the happy confluence of new printing technology and a burgeoning publishing industry responding to the demands of eager readers added a golden aura to the period from the 1890s to the 1930s.

AT THE OAKS

Parrish married Lydia Austin, a fellow artist, in 1895. As an enchanted public demanded more of his work, the child in Parrish was eclipsed by the hermit. In 1898, he retreated to his own slice of paradise. On a hill across the valley from his father's home looking out at Vermont's Mount Ascutney, Parrish built the Oaks. By the time it was finished in 1906, the estate boasted a twenty-room main house and a fifteen-room studio, complete with a darkroom and machine shop.

During his first decade at the Oaks, Parrish was astonishingly versatile and widely praised. He did murals, shipping the painted panels to hotels in New York, Chicago and San Francisco. He illustrated *The Arabian Nights* and Nathaniel Hawthorne's *Tanglewood Tales*, and his stunning landscapes accompanied *Italian Villas and Their Gardens* by Edith Wharton. He even found time to paint scenery for a Broadway production of Shakespeare's *The Tempest*. At the Oaks, Maxfield and Lydia Parrish enjoyed the community of the arts at Cornish's thriving artist's colony, where dinner guests included the sculptor Augustus Saint Gardens, Ethel Barrymore and Woodrow Wilson. The community staged annual dramas with sets and masks by Parrish. In time, Parrish began to complement his works of internal fantasy with fantastical outdoor panoramas graced by the woman who served as his muse.

Maxfield Parrish women often seem to be the same woman. In fact, many of them are. Her name was Susan Lewin, and she came to the Oaks to help Lydia care for the children when she was only sixteen. Parrish soon asked Susan to pose for him. He rarely painted from life; instead, he preferred photographing his models and working from his own prints. Over time, with Lydia wintering in Georgia, Parrish and his model began a relationship that lasted fifty-five years. Lewin's room in the Oaks was connected to Parrish's by a secret passage, and in 1911, she and Parrish moved into his studio while Lydia stayed in the main house. With Susan posing, Parrish's dreamscapes matured.

On the heels of the 1913 Armory Show in Chicago, which exposed Americans to Picasso and other modern greats, critics proclaimed that a painting no longer had to be pretty, just personal. Parrish became the anti-

Matisse, a painter of pleasing pictures for the masses. Weary of the commercial game, Parrish tried other markets, yet the public demanded more of the same from him. Rather than renounce the income that let him live on his hilltop, he painted paradise continuously. In the 1920s, his prints made him the highest-paid artist in America. More than seventeen million Maxfield Parrish calendars fed the public's hunger for his blend of the exotic and the erotic.

DAYBREAK

As the nation accelerated into the 1920s, Parrish continued to be part of the cultural landscape. In his short story "May Day," F. Scott Fitzgerald called a window's reflection "a deep, creamy blue, the color of Maxfield Parrish Moonlight." Hoping to become more than a cliché, Parrish began dreaming of greater things. The result was *Daybreak*, and it became, in the words of a Parrish biographer, "the decorating sensation of the decade." *Daybreak* sold more than 200,000 prints. The buyer of *Daybreak* swore the gallery to secrecy, and so, as it became one of the most reproduced artworks in history, no one knew where the original hung. The mystery went unsolved for nearly a half century. Then, in 1974, the painting surfaced at a Boston gallery. *Daybreak*'s buyer had been politician William Jennings Bryan, the grandfather of its reclining model, Kitty Owen.

Among Parrish collectors are film stars Jack Nicholson and Whoopi Goldberg, as well as that master of his own brand of make believe, *Star Wars* creator George Lucas.

LON MEGARGEE: COWBOY ARTIST

There is always that hidden spark if we are fortunate enough to find it that transforms the hideous into the beautiful.

Often branded as Arizona's original cowboy artist, Megargee's work links the history and art of the state with which he wanted to be most identified. He nurtured an image of himself as a cowboy artist in the tradition established by Charles M. Russell and Frederick Remington.

The restlessly independent Megargee certainly became one of the best-known cowboy artists. His paintings introduced the state's spectacular landscape and its native people to a wide audience, helping forge the image of Arizona as it exists today. In that sense, he was truly a pioneer. Though he was born in Philadelphia in 1883, he would later claim Tombstone as his birthplace. In the mid-1920s, in Taos, New Mexico, the artist spent considerable time painting and making contacts to further his career.

Megaregee was as good at image making as his art—being western was part of the myth he created, painted and personified for much of his lifetime. After attending one of Buffalo Bill Cody's Wild West shows, Megargee made up his mind to become a cowboy. At age thirteen, he moved to Arizona, and by the time he was twenty-four, he was the foreman of a ranch north of Phoenix. He was a stunt roper, broncobuster and saloon poker dealer. His first trip to paint en plein-air was to the land of Hopi and Navajo people in northern Arizona.

What Megargee put on canvas were his dreams, a peculiar blend of real-life cowboy experience and his boyhood imaginings, flavored by pulp fiction. Megargee was perpetually on the move, often running from women and their lawyers and broke. His commercial paintings were also popular. For many Arizonans his most famous work is the *Cowboy's Dream*, one of four paintings he made for A-1 Beer, the Phoenix-based Arizona Brewing Company, which became highly successful promotional posters, and he created several designs for Stetson Hat Company. He had a restless intellect that pulled him in many creative directions. He wrote songs; dabbled in architecture, designing several homes in Phoenix, Cave Creek and Sedona; and did a stint as an art director at Paramount Studios in Hollywood. Arizona is where he staked his name, however. Some of his familiar subjects include the Grand Canyon, the Petrified Forest, Canyon de Chelly, the San Francisco Peaks and Mission San Xavier.

Perhaps author Oren Arnold put it best when he wrote that Megargee's paintings were not meant to be hung "in Aunt Minnie's sitting room or in the Y.W.C.A....rather they were appropriate for an adobe house, pine lodge or dude ranch." In 1960, Megaregee was living in Sedona in a house overlooking Oak Creek when he suffered a fatal heart attack. His ashes were scattered by airplane over what was the Billy Cook Ranch, where he'd worked as a foreman many years before.

EUGENIA EVERETT: SCULPTOR

Even if it is not bringing you a name, or bringing you money, or anything of that kind, it still has its value because life is the important thing.

Eugenia Everett was a sculptor who had worked in many media including bronze, concrete, wood and marble, always experimenting with new ideas. Born in Loveland, Colorado, in 1908, she moved with her family to California, residing in San Diego, Los Angeles and then Ojai in 1938. When Everett entered the Otis Art Institute in Los Angeles in the 1930s, she chose sculpture over painting, and a career of over sixty years blossomed, beginning with work through the Federal Art Project.

> *At the time I went to Otis it was different from what it is now. You could go and take anything you wanted to take. There were no credits, no degrees, and they didn't require anything at all. But I was so involved in sculpture and so interested in it that I wouldn't take anything else. I didn't take drawing or painting or anything else. Later I more or less regretted it in a certain way because I thought that I should have had that training in that. And I have had fun at times in my life when I couldn't really work, opening up another field by taking a little painting. I started the pottery actually at a time when I didn't feel I could do sculpture.*

She took a hiatus to raise her family in Ojai, California, saying later,

> *I have the feeling that one of the articles written about me at the time of the Project was very prophetic. The title of it was, "Gifted Sculptress Prefers Life to Career"…I feel that I've had life but I haven't had a career. I haven't any complaints because I feel that art which doesn't grow out of life has no value anyhow. And I wouldn't give up life for art. But art is a wonderful crowning part of life if you can have it at the time….Nobody has as much of it as they want. Even if you have only a moment of it, or a short time of it, one thing a completion, it is worthwhile.*

After a move to Sedona, she taught and exhibited at the Sedona Arts Center for many years as a beloved teacher. Resuming her career brought many commissions and the production of high-value art, including a monument at the Oxnard California Performing Arts Center; a Stations of the Cross at St. Daniel the Prophet church in Scottsdale; *Celebration*

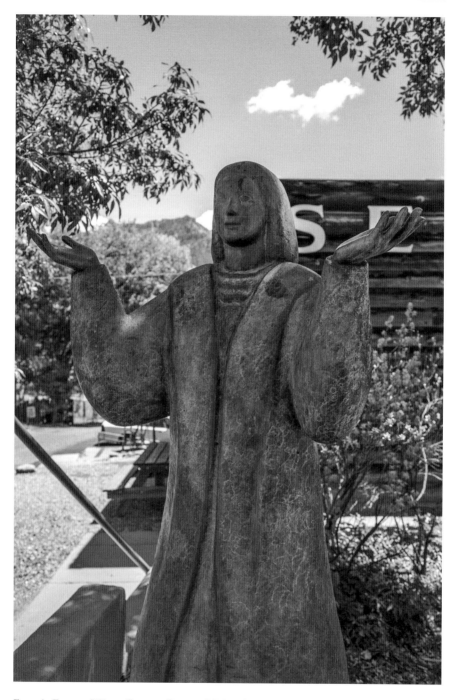

Eugenia Everett. *Welcome*. Bronze. *Courtesy of Sedona Chamber of Commerce & Tourism Bureau.*

and *Aria* in Sedona, commissioned by Gardens for Humanity; and many others. Everett is known for her combination of the realistic and abstract, representational and nonobjective. "Everett is an artist of life. She doesn't stick to just one medium, or just one subject. She rambles, as does the spirit, through the sands of time," wrote reviewer Nancy Robb Dunst. She was a great fan of Henry Moore, the English artist and sculptor. She believed that in order for a sculpture to be properly appreciated it must be properly displayed, so her work can be found in museums, galleries and private collections all over the country.

Everett's daughter Edson W. Kempe reflects on her mother's legacy:

> *Eugenia was so dear to me in that identity that I was not as aware as I should have been until late in her life just how good she was, and how great a teacher. She did not really have time for her art while I was growing up and she was teaching high school, helping to run our family resort, and raising me and my brother. My husband's career was in the Foreign Service, we retired on Orcas Island, and her time with us during that period was devoted to sharing our experiences and locations much more than hers.*

Everett's philosophy on art as much as her work give us a glimpse of the spirit and character behind her accomplishments as an artist: "The process is more important than selling the product. The result and what led up to it mattered; not so much whether it sold. But it did."

JOE BEELER: COWBOY ARTIST

As a western genre painter and sculptor, Joe Beeler became one of the nation's most prolific and best-known western artists in the late twentieth century. Born in Joplin, Missouri, in 1931, Beeler grew up in northeastern Oklahoma, where all he ever wanted to do was be a cowboy and draw pictures.

After graduating from high school, he attended junior college for a time, worked on a cattle ranch in Arizona and, in 1950, entered the University of Tulsa. There he studied art for two years under Alexandre Hogue. In 1952, he enrolled at the University of Missouri, but his academic career was cut short when he was drafted into the U.S. Army during the Korean War. While serving, he drew cartoons for several service newspapers, including *Stars and Stripes*. Upon being discharged from the army, he utilized the GI Bill to earn a bachelor of fine arts degree from Kansas State University in 1957. He followed this with a year of study at the Los Angeles Art Center. Unlike those who received their calling later in life, Joe Beeler always knew he was an artist—he could always draw, it just came naturally. Beeler was strongly influenced toward western art because of his own heritage. His father was part Cherokee, so Joe was raised with deep respect for the Indian customs. In addition, his family friends shared with him the stories of the early pioneers, the Civil War, the gold rush and more.

In 1958, he returned to northeastern Oklahoma, where he lived in a cabin in a remote location near Quapaw, in Ottawa County, and concentrated on painting. In late 1958, he received his first professional commission by doing book illustrations for the University of Oklahoma Press. The following year, he had a one-man exhibition at the Gilcrease Institute of American Art (now Gilcrease Museum) in Tulsa. Following this exhibition, demand for both his paintings and magazine illustrations increased to the point that in 1961, he moved to Sedona to be closer to the center of interest of the fledgling western art world. Four years later, he expanded his artistic range to include sculpture.

A deep love for the western tradition, combined with his artistic ability, has taken Beeler to the top of his profession. As both a painter and sculptor, Beeler excelled, and his rare dual talent was widely recognized and honored. Over the years, he received numerous accolades, including numerous CAA gold and silver medals. His work is displayed in the finest western art museums and galleries throughout the nation, and his name is a household word among western art enthusiasts.

HELEN FRANKENTHALER: ABSTRACT EXPRESSIONIST

One of the foremost painters of the mid-twentieth century, Frankenthaler first painted works based on her visits to Arizona in 1977, creating pieces such as *Sedona* (1977) and *Indian Redscape* (1977). In these pieces Sedona's majestic red cliffs and expanses of high desert scenery captivate the viewer, all of which Frankenthaler was able to capture beautifully in her format. In Frankenthaler's desire to capture, in particular, Sedona red, she took rock samples from the area from her initial visit in 1976 back to her studio in order to re-create the exact color. In these two works is represented a movement that Frankenthaler pioneered: color field painting.

Introduced early in her career to artists such as Jackson Pollock and Franz Kline, Frankenthaler was influenced by Abstract Expressionist painting practices but developed her own distinct approach to the style. She invented the "soak-stain" technique, in which she poured turpentine-thinned paint onto canvas, producing luminous color washes that seemed to merge with the canvas and negate any hint of three-dimensional illusionism. Her breakthrough approach gave rise to a movement endorsed by the persuasive art critic Clement Greenberg as the "next big thing" in American art: color field painting, a movement marked by airy compositions that celebrated the joys of pure color and gave an entirely new look and feel to the surface of the canvas. The stain process is spontaneous due to the unpredictability of the exact edge that may develop between color masses.

Later in her career, Frankenthaler turned her attention to other creative media endeavors, most notably woodcuts, in which she achieved quality of painting, in some cases replicating the effects of the soak-stain process.

JOHN HENRY WADDELL: SCULPTOR

A love of mankind is the thrust of famed artist John Waddell's work, and sculpture became his primary art form. Waddell was born in Des Moines, Iowa; attended the Art Institute of Chicago; and had his first solo show in Peoria, Illinois, at age twenty-one. He was in the military, and the GI Bill financed the remainder of his formal education, which were two MFAs in fine arts and art education. In 1957, he and his wife, Ruth, a close partner in his professional as well as his personal life, moved to Arizona, where he headed the art education department at Arizona State University for several years. Phoenix has received an abundance of outdoor sculpture, largely the work of Waddell.

In 1961, Waddell took a two-year leave to work in Mexico. After a year back on campus at ASU, he completely forsook academic security to spend three years with his family in Greece, the cradle of Western sculpture, before settling at the very geographical heart of Arizona, the Verde Valley, in 1970. Throughout these moves, Waddell has had the support of Ruth, also an artist in her own right. By the warmth of his personality, a persistent dedication to his art and the quality of his work, Waddell has been able to attract patrons to fund the costly materials needed for bronze casting.

Waddell took the extraordinary step of incorporating himself and selling shares in his future to a few Phoenicians. First among them was the banker

Walter Bimson, a well-known philanthropist for the arts. Bimson backed his liking of Waddell's work for himself and for the headquarters and branches of the Valley National Bank. But it was the late Louise Kerr of Phoenix, a gifted composer, who was responsible for Waddell's settling in the Verde Valley. She admired his work done in Greece, and when he returned, she offered him sanctuary on her ranch on Spring Creek. There, on a portion that he now owns, Waddell used money from the sale of his work to establish a master apprentice fellowship program that would combine creativity and instruction. When Waddell first came over Mingus Mountain, which walls the Verde Valley in the west, he said that he looked down on this valley and sensed that it would be his final place.

In *Dance*, a grouping of twelve bronze nude dancers in the Phoenix Civic Plaza, he pays homage to this humanism. In Tucson, another of his sculptures celebrates the body—the lithe figures of nude female flute players have charmed onlookers outside the University of Arizona main library since the 1970s.

Waddell's reverence for the human body is evident in his grasp of anatomical drawing—such mastery is part of all great artists' repertoire whether in sculpture or painting. At age forty-three, he resigned from teaching to become a full-time sculptor. Waddell is best known for bronze sculptures of female nudes in motion. This process, this touching and exploring the flesh of the corresponding model, is a break from tradition. Sculptors aren't taught this method in school. Among his models were his wife, their grandson and Russian author Leo Tolstoy's great-granddaughter, a friend of Waddell's.

Waddell's sculptures include *Expulsion from the Garden of the Earth*, *Circle of Womanhood* and *Celebration*. With a timeless quality like the work of Michelangelo of Florence or Rodin in Paris, the figures are without clothing. Thus they are not dated by the transient nature of style. Among the fourteen sculptures, an age range between seventeen months and seventy-five years is depicted. Although each is very individualistic, they are connected by this common theme of humanity.

But perhaps his most significant and political piece memorializes the 1963 church bombing in Birmingham, Alabama, in which four young girls died, becoming a pivotal event in his development as an artist. The monument he created in response to that tragedy, a group of cast figures called *That Which Might Have Been, Birmingham, 1963*, resides in the garden he designed for it at the Unitarian Universalist Church on Lincoln Drive in Phoenix. When he and his family were returning from

John Henry Waddell's twelve bronze figures, *The Dance*, are assembled at his Cornville studio. *Courtesy of Sedona Historical Society.*

Mexico, they heard of the bombing on the radio. Waddell was deeply shocked; his anger turned to sorrow. To memorialize the tragedy in some lasting way, he conceived portraying the girls in the maturity denied them, a monument "to the beauty of individual differences," in hopes of countering such senseless violence. None of the figures is alike, and yet all illustrate the sculptor's thesis that a society attains its highest level when it appreciates the many faces of beauty.

A part of the Arizona art world for more than fifty years, Waddell has been teaching and exhibiting his work, both in one-man shows and in permanent displays, throughout the state. His work has been acquired and displayed countrywide from the Mondavi Vineyards in Napa Valley,

John Henry Waddell works on dancing figures for Phoenix Civic Plaza. *Courtesy of Sedona Historical Society.*

California, to the Flushing Meadows Tennis Center in New York City. It is also present in public venues in Phoenix, including the Civic Plaza, Art Museum, Herberger Theatre and the Sedona Cultural Park.

DAVE SANTILLANES: LANDSCAPE PAINTER

"I'm always intrigued by simple, abstract designs in the landscape, how light and shadow fall on the landscape, sometimes its atmospheric elements that simplify a design. There's no better teacher than nature for capturing these elusive elements," says Dave Santillanes, a multi–award winning oil painter from Fort Collins, Colorado, specializing in plein-air and studio landscapes, who frequently finds himself in Sedona. "When I'm painting outdoors I'm inspired by the entire experience—the visual and the spiritual," the modest, effervescent painter explains. "My aim is merely to capture the essence of the scene before me, but in doing that, I hope my reverence for the land also comes through."

It is the meditative part of plein-air painting that appeals to Santillanes the most. "For me it's more than just getting a finished painting…so many things happen when you setup to paint and intensely observe a scene for a couple of hours." During this process, you become a stationary object and a part of the landscape. "I've had intimate encounters with bear, moose, elk, all while painting." Hiking in, planning, painting and hiking out would characterize a typical day for the artist.

Santillanes's interpretation of nature has a particular influence on how people perceive their surroundings. Awakened to their surroundings, fans remark that they didn't realize they lived in such a beautiful place until they saw it through the eyes of an artist. "I was painting a ridge above a residential community. I liked how the light was hitting the ridge creating some nice atmosphere and abstract patterns. At the opening of the plein-air event three different couples from the community wanted to purchase the painting."

Though a resident of Colorado, Santillanes remains inspired by Arizona's land, light and color. "Particularly the Sedona Verde Valley is a unique and exotic landscape. The opportunities for big shapes and abstract designs abound."

CURT WALTERS: ACTIVIST AND PLEIN-AIR IMPRESSIONIST

I simply respond to all things beautiful. Like most artists, I find color and beauty in most everything and everybody.

Plein-air is the only way a landscape painter can create and develop great work, according to artist Curt Walters of Sedona, Arizona, best known as a plein-air Impressionist.

Walters is world renowned for his flawless interpretation of the Grand Canyon. *Art of the West* magazine called him the "Greatest Living Grand Canyon Artist," and many museums and collectors don't feel their collections are complete unless they include a Walters painting.

Walters's career is notable for his weighty presence in southwestern art. Walters was chosen to paint the Grand Canyon for the seventy-fifth anniversary rededication ceremonies in 1994. The Nor Este Subdivision in Albuquerque, New Mexico, dubbed one of its streets Curt Walters Court in recognition of his contributions to the arts in the Land of Enchantment.

Each year, his artwork can be seen at many of America's top western art shows, the most prominent of them being an exceptional run at the Prix de West exhibition at the National Cowboy and Western Heritage Museum in Oklahoma City. Walters has received great acclaim at these exhibitions, bringing home more than a dozen awards over the past decade. Though he has many accomplishments, winning the Prix de West purchase award in 2007 when the National Cowboy Museum acquired his work *Spring's Caprice* was a thirty-year goal achieved.

Walters's passion to create is lifelong. At the age of fifteen, Walters sold his first piece. Finding almost all art from all cultures and time periods fascinating, he has discovered that the center of his aesthetics lie with the art produced from 1850 to the 1930s. "I am as fond of the architecture as I am of the visual arts of this period of Early Modernism, particularly Monet and Sargent."

Before he was twenty years old, the fledgling young artist visited the Grand Canyon for the first time, and so began a lasting love affair. Since those early years, Walters has focused much of his time and energies on the site—and not only as an artist. In the early 1990s, the growing amount of air pollution over the gorge (something unintentionally documented within his paintings) began to concern Walters. Shortly thereafter, he became aware of the Grand Canyon Trust's efforts to fight pollution's damaging effects throughout the entire Colorado Plateau. "As my knowledge and interest in the subject grew, I found I could use my art to support the foundation's fight to protect Grand Canyon from air pollution."

Walters was inspired to donate his work, resulting in the raising of over $500,000 toward this cause. For his hard work and dedication, he was honored as "Official Artist of the Grand Canyon Trust." In 1999, Walters put together fourteen like-minded artist friends and took a rafting trip down the Colorado River through the Grand Canyon. They painted along the way, and this resulted in a show and sale at Forbes Magazine Galleries in New York City. The proceeds of show went to the Grand Canyon Trust.

Walters never was the "protest type," he says, but things change. "I believe it is the role of any artist to bring awareness to every nook and cranny of society. I think many artists throughout history have social agendas and political agendas within their work. I don't think the great artists stopped

Cody DeLong. *Around the Bend*. Oil on canvas. 2013. *Artist's collection.*

Cody DeLong. *Flat Iron 2*. Oil on canvas. 2014. *Artist's collection.*

Cody DeLong. *Jerome After Sundown*. Oil on canvas. 2013. *Artist's collection.*

Cody DeLong. *Mile High Life*. Oil on canvas. 2013. *Artist's collection.*

Cody DeLong. *Retirement Home*. Oil on canvas. 2014. *Artist's collection.*

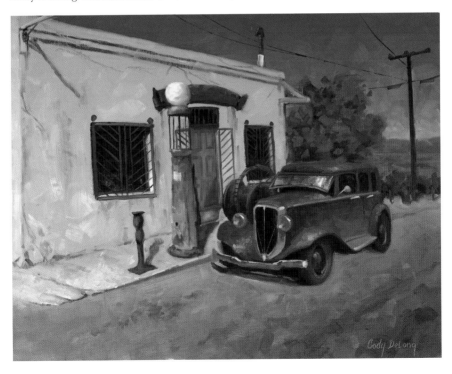

Cody DeLong. *Studebaker*. Oil on canvas. 2013. *Artist's collection.*

Birgitta Lapides. *Ascent.* Mixed Media. 2007. *Artist's collection.*

Birgitta Lapides. *Arizona Landscape 14.* Mixed-media collage. 2009. *Artist's collection.*

Birgitta Lapides. *Arizona Landscape 19.* Mixed-media collage. 2011. *Artist's collection.*

Right: Birgitta Lapides. *Musical Inspiration*. Mixed-media collage. 2008. *Artist's collection.*

Below: Dave Santillanes. *Daybreak at Cedar Ridge*. Oil. 2014. *Artist's collection.*

Jan Sitts. *Radiating Teal*. Thirty by forty. Mixed Media. Acrylic on canvas. 2014. *Artist's collection.*

"Merlin" 10 ft. High

John M.Soderberg, *Merlin*. Patinaed bronze. *Artist's collection.*

Qiang Huang. *Cathedral Rock*. Oil on board. 2013.
Artist's collection.

Joella Jean Mahoney. *Lone Mesa, High Wind*. Southwest Landscape Series. Oil on canvas.
1984. *Artist's collection.*

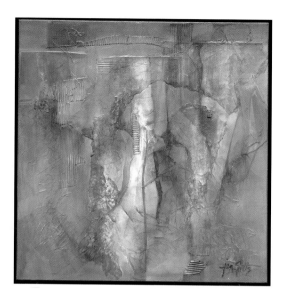

Jan Sitts. *It's in the Greens.* Mixed media acrylic on canvas. 2012. *Artist's collection.*

Ellen Jo Roberts. *Clark Mansion*. Acrylic on canvas. *2011. Artist's collection.*

Above: Ellen Jo Roberts.
Cottonwood Arizona.
Acrylic on canvas.
2011. Artist's collection.

Right: Ellen Jo Roberts.
Sycamore Canyon.
Acrylic on canvas.
2011. Artist's collection.

Above: Ellen Jo Roberts. *Vintage Jerome.* Acrylic on canvas. Painted in 2012 in honor of the state centennial. *Artist's collection.*

Right: Curt Walters. *First Touch of Winter.* Oil on canvas. 2013. This piece won the Fredrick Remington Painting Award at the 2013 Prix de West Invitational, National Cowboy Museum. *Artist's collection.*

Right: Maxfield Parrish. *Arizona.*
Oil on canvas. 1930. *Art* ©
Maxfield Parrish Family, LLC/
Licensed by VAGA, New York.

Opposite: Joella Jean Mahoney. *Kayenta Canyon.* Cleft Series. Oil on canvas. 1982. *Artist's collection.*

Joella Jean Mahoney. *Mystery Ridge.* Southwest Landscape Series. Oil on canvas. 1978. *Artist's collection.*

Dave Santillanes. *Oak Creek Canyon.* Oil. 2014. *Artist's collection*

Mark Rownd. *Desert Music*. Oil on wood. 2014. *Artist's collection.*

Bernie Lopez. *Sedona Moon*. Acrylic on canvas. 2014. *Artist's collection.*

Chapel of the Holy Cross. Library of Congress, Prints & Photographs Division, photograph by Carol M. Highsmith.

Howard Carr. *Little Pinky*. Oil on canvas. 2014. *Artist's collection.*

Howard Carr. *River Jewels*. Oil on canvas. 2014. *Artist's collection.*

and said, 'Let's just paint a pretty picture.' I know I love using my paintings in ways that go beyond just the act of painting."

Walters cannot help placing contemporary issues of the West in his art, though not overtly. Often behind the simple landscape is his personal, deeper story, which can symbolize many things, population expansion and air quality issues, for example. The artist has stayed close to the trust and the Grand Canyon Foundation. "My long-term goal is to see the development of a fine arts museum at Grand Canyon National Park."

However, it is doubtful that the public at large "gets" the deeper meanings behind Walters's paintings. What attract the viewer to his works are their subject matter, color and good composition. "The viewer's experience is rarely what my own intention was with a work...those artists that survive the test of time are those who have painted their own time; contemporary issues whether on the surface or symbolically included in the artist's own way are always found in art."

While his American travels have taken Walters to some of the world's most exotic locations around the globe, it is in the landscape of Arizona where Walters feels most comfortable. The geographic diversity is amazing, he says, alpine to canyons to desert. What keeps him in Sedona, specifically, are the people—"people here are continually interesting."

Walters's artwork can be found at the Trailside Galleries of Scottsdale, Arizona, and Jackson, Wyoming, and in Vail, Colorado. His work is collected among a number of public and private individuals and foundations, including the Forbes Magazine Galleries of New York and California, Kareem Abdul-Jabbar, astronaut Frank Borman, Frank and Kathie Lee Gifford and (of course) Grand Canyon National Park. Walters is currently working on a historical project, he mysteriously adds with a twinkle in his eyes. "It will be unlike anything else I've painted, and I am looking forward to the challenge of new subject matters."

BETTY CARR: WATERCOLORIST

I try to capture the feeling that something just happened or is about to happen in the painting.

Betty Carr was born and raised in Santa Cruz, California, and developed a love of art from visiting museums. In 1980, she married landscape painter Howard Carr, and they have devoted their lives to painting, traveling several months each year from Oregon to Southern Carolina in a specially equipped mobile home. Following years of instructing art in Colorado and California and developing her distinctive painting style, Betty, along with Howard, decided to follow the sun to the Southwest, where color and light are ever present.

Energetic, brightly colored still life is the signature work of this artist, known for skillful use of light, color and shadow that accentuate her subject matter while showing her love of nature and its forms.

As early as she can remember, Carr's love for creating has been present. The most important subject in her early education was art—drawing, painting and sculpture. Outside the classroom, early exposure to great art through many trips to various art museums played an important role in her passion to achieve excellence in art. The best of each artistic era has influenced Carr's directions; Surrealism, Impressionism, post-Impressionism and more, but her "first love" derives from the years surrounding the Renaissance. Studying the works of Titian, Leonardo da Vinci, Vermeer and Caravaggio affected her direction in painting and sculpting. "Chiaroscuro, dramatic light and dark really became instilled in my work and inspired [me] to write my book on light, *Seeing the Light*, an artist's guide."

Carr has emerged as one of the foremost painters of the Southwest. From the time she was a young girl, Carr has been represented by galleries. She has been featured in numerous publications, including *Art of the West*, *Southwest Art*, *American Artist*, *Art Talk*, *American Artist* and *Vitality* magazines. Since gaining a master's degree from San Jose State University in California, Betty has taught painting, drawing and sculpture at primary, secondary and college levels and has developed a following through both private and workshop instruction. She advises her students to draw continually since drawing is critical to good painting.

On the influence of light on her watercolors, she comments, "What catches my eye is the effect light has on form in unique situations, whether fleeting, spilling over, striking. I challenge myself in capturing its dramatic and/or subtle effects. The spontaneous qualities lend itself perfectly to my Impressionistic style of painting. I strive for confident enthusiastic brushwork, the maximizing of color's value and intensity range and a fresh painterly approach, the result appearing effortless."

Most of Carr's paintings are inspired by nature's bounty and are enveloped in unique lighting situations—early morning light with long shadows, sparkling snow shadows, glowing fields before dusk. "I hope to convey this emotion I feel to the viewer." She adds, more broadly, that this positive emotion in approach helps society carry on with greater optimism.

It is this very openness that may be what draws people to her work. Carr shows her work in a number of galleries around the nation in Jackson, Wyoming; Calistoga, California; and Santa Fe. "In annual collector exhibitions, many collectors come back every year at shows to see new pieces while others drop in my galleries to check out what's new," says Carr. Fortunately, she has developed a large collector base after painting for many years.

Carr strives to capture the mood, or essence, of a scene with spontaneous, painterly brushwork that appears effortless, striving for brevity above all else. "I want the viewer to sense this passion and excitement I felt while creating the painting." Many of her most favorite works have been plein-air works painted on location in and around the state of Arizona. "Every aspect of the landscape, folks, serve as inspiration—the openness of the terrain and diversity of painting material, from unique mining towns, architectural settings and of course the fantastic jaw-dropping red rocks and canyons."

Carr is extremely proud of her acceptance into the exclusive Knickerbocker Association of New York City and as a master in the American Impressionist Society and the Arizona Plein Air Painters. She is collected both privately and corporately and has been accepted in numerous juried exhibitions.

Like her contemporaries, Carr is captured by the beauty and multiple resources for paintings along the Verde River, in old Cottonwood, in the town of Jerome and, of course, from the incredible Red Rocks of Sedona. "It's an artist's paradise that can't be beat," Carr says. Carr has been focusing on Arizona vineyard paintings as of late. During the Sedona Plein-Air Festival in October, her painting *Autumn Vineyard* won the prestigious award of "A Confluence of the Senses" from Alcantara Vineyards and the Sedona Art Center. The painting will be used as a label for their new blend in spring.

HOWARD CARR: IMPRESSIONIST

Light is what creates color and color is painting

Howard Carr earned his art degree at Chouinard Art School and a fine arts degree from the California College of Arts and Crafts. Nothing inspires Carr more than light on any subject or scene whether it is a dramatic, bright contrast or a dull fog rolling across a valley. Focusing on simple abstract shapes catching the light in certain areas, Carr studies the hidden colors and values present in nature (and his imagination), presenting the essence of the color and mood simply by focusing on the important parts of the painting. In elementary school, Carr drew everything, intrigued by the challenge of making things more interesting through distorting and adding color in more interesting and unique ways. Born in California, when he was eight, Carr got involved in acting, landing roles in several television series, including *The Rifleman*, *My Three Sons* and *The Danny Thomas Show.*

Using large brushstrokes, Carr is a true Impressionist painting the subjects of people at work and play, the stuff of daily life. In taking in all subjects, he works at capturing the effect of light on the subject. It was the artist Sorolla who captured Carr's attention with his Spanish coastal scenes of fishing boats and children at play on the beach. "I'd like the viewer to feel the subtle atmospheric elements as well as the movement, sometimes very dynamic, in my work."

Today, Carr's wants as a professional artist are modest—to be able to wake up each day inspired and passionate with a cup of coffee in his hands. Nonetheless, Carr is constantly coming up with new ideas of how to handle the subject and medium in a way that is truly his own. "You might say I paint my own numbers." He has recently been excited about the subject of busy chefs and staff in a restaurant or street café, perhaps with the kitchen full of steam and flames and all the commotion. "There is a lot going on behind those swinging doors. Painting on location at these places requires a fast brush."

Carr exhibits in galleries throughout Scottsdale; Richmond, Virginia; and Santa Fe, New Mexico. "I'll always be a painter," he says. "The Verde Valley is located in the middle of endless subject matter to get spoiled with; I see a big art community happening here soon. So hang on to your hat."

CODY DELONG: PLEIN-AIR AND STUDIO PAINTER

Jerome-based studio and plein-air artist, the multi–award winning Cody de Long exudes extraordinary modesty. Much of his glorious work is indicative of and inspired by the sights and character of the town of Jerome—the historic streets and panoramic views. What each of his pieces beautifully captures is the light. But never one to dwell on his accomplishments, DeLong's next piece is always his most meaningful, he says.

While DeLong worked in airbrushing in Las Vegas, he kept passing by the Verde Valley area and was immediately drawn to its spectacular beauty. Spending time as a plein-air artist around the valley, DeLong noticed Jerome's authentically small-town character and the historic district quaintness where so much is unchanged; the little artist's colony invaded his thoughts.

The community of Jerome has worked hard to develop into one dedicated to the arts. "We've grown that reputation over the years as a diverse art destination," says DeLong. DeLong loves being out in the natural world on the outskirts of town, where he can interpret nature, just as equally—he finds there is an "underlying abstract quality to representational landscape painting." He alternates working from a photograph or a study painted on site. "Each painting I do begins with an idea, something that's inspired me. I try to distill this into my own abstract design and interpretation of nature. The balance I'm searching for lies in creating a work that is technically proficient as well as 'painterly,' with great color and sense of light and drama."

Having studied at the Loveland Academy of Fine Arts, as well as the Scottsdale Artists School, DeLong has received a lengthy list of plein-air-related awards and was invited to participate in the Plein-Air on the Rim portion of the inaugural Celebration of Art at the Grand Canyon in 2009. He was one of twenty artists from across the country invited to participate and has been each year since. He has also been a top seller every year and, in 2012, was the top-selling artist at the Grand Canyon.

DeLong and his work has been featured in many art magazines, including the covers of *Sedona Magazine*, *Western Art Collector*, *American Artist Workshop Magazine*, *Arizona Highways*, *Southwest Art*, *Sedona Monthly*, *Phoenix Magazine*, *Mountain Living Magazine* and *Southwest Art Magazine*. The artist is a co-founding member of Arizona Plein-Air Painters Association.

BIRGITTA LAPIDES: ABSTRACT AND LANDSCAPE PAINTER

Freshness of vision and originality of concept are fundamental to my identity as artist.

What inspires Swedish-born Lapides first and foremost is nature. She will tell you, "I love the landscape here, the sky, the light and the colors." Her work "comes from some kind of accumulated inspiration of just being surrounded by all the beauty here in Arizona."

I asked Lapides about her artistic process; she refers to herself as an "intuitive painter, one who paints entirely from imagination—never from photos. For me, colors, textures and forms are the most important elements in a painting, although I always feel inspired by the beauty of the landscape around me."

In working on her collage landscapes, she typically paints the sky first and then paints "a lot of thin, thin papers" that she tears up and uses in her painting. For added inspiration, Lapides plays classical music and then gets absorbed in the process. "It's a journey of discovery and adventure for me." When it comes to her abstract paintings, it becomes more difficult for her to explain how she arrives at the finished product. "Sometimes I just use paint, but mostly I mix collage and paintings." Above all, for Lapides, painting is a solitary experience; she just has to listen to her inner voice.

Lapides's life story is utterly fascinating. She grew up in a little town on the Baltic Sea in Sweden, about forty-five minutes northeast of Stockholm, and has always been involved in art in some form. In Sweden, she loved oil painting but also worked with clay. The fine arts have always been an integral part of her life.

She married young and moved to France with her Swedish husband and three-year-old daughter, Mia. They lived in a very beautiful area outside Geneva on the French side. "My son Emile was born in France, and with two small children, I did not have time for any art work." Lapides lived and worked many years as a weaver in France before coming to United States. Her love for texture started as a weaver: "It was as a weaver and clothing designer for many years—first in Sweden, then in Belgium and France and finally in the United States, that I learned the supreme importance of color and texture."

Lapides began formal art education at L'École Supérieure D'Architecture et Art Appliqué (La Cambre) in Brussels in 1977 and finished in 1979. She continued studies at the Pratt Institute in New York City, receiving her degree in textile design in 1982. Her children only spoke French when they arrived to New York, and so "we had a lot of adjustment to do, both my children and myself. But we got to love New York with all the culture, museums and all kinds of exhibitions. I remember that I saw an exhibition with Kurt Schwitter's collage at the Museum of Modern Art, and I got really interested in collage making."

At Pratt, Lapides's favorite classes were screen printing, and she studied dark room technics for screen printers with two Japanese teachers, who taught her how to develop photographs and use them in screen printing. The process inspired a show in New York. After Lapides finished Pratt, she decided to return to France. "I ended up renting a place in Frejus, which is between Cannes and St. Tropez. My place was in old town, and I rented it from the Culture Department; my landlord was the French Culture minister at that time. I had a store and shop and workspace in the very old part of town and an apartment upstairs. The building was from Roman times, and in the stairs I even had an inscription from a Roman slave who thanked his owner for letting him free. The basement had been an old Roman bath."

Lapides studied drawing and painting at the École des Beaux-Arts in Cannes, where she displayed work at a group show at the Palais des Festivals. She also had one-artist shows in New York City and in Jerome, Arizona.

> *While living for many years in France (where Provence meets the Riviera), I operated my own studio and workshop, where I sold hand-woven jackets of my design. The brilliant colors of sea, sky and earth along the Mediterranean entered indelibly into my creative imagination.*
>
> *Those years were very interesting and I learned a lot about surviving in a new way. I met a lot of different people and, among them, a lot of rich Swedes [who] lived six months and one day on the French Riviera to avoid Swedish taxes and the rest of the year in Sweden. But most of all, it was very, very hard work.*

In 1993, Lapides married her current husband, Kenny, from New York City, and they moved to Vermont. After having lived for so long on the French Riviera, Lapides was willing to move anywhere it was sunny, so they arrived to Arizona.

The fabulous palette of Arizona's earth and sky has been a good change for the artist, inspiring her in both her landscape and nonrepresentational (abstract) painting. "My art is an act of homage to the gifts of nature and to the wonders of the imagination…I continue to study with well-known artists in workshops held in Sedona, Arizona, and regard my own evolving work in painting and collage as the essence of my journey through life," she says.

When not painting, she finds ways to be creative in other areas—including creating hand-painted earrings to sell in different galleries and making pendants in polymer clay. "To be creative is a journey of discovery…That's why I don't like to paint after photographs—I don't want to know the end result. I go with flow and discover new things."

Lapides's methods are working for her, and she has sold to collectors from all over the world. It is this deep drive to be creative and love of color and texture that keep her going as an artist. A typical day for Lapides begins extremely early, usually four o'clock in the morning. "I take an early brisk walk around the three lagoons in Dead Horse State Park. After lunch I take siesta, something I got into habit [of] from southern France [where] most people take siesta after lunch. Later in the afternoon, I take my dog Leo [a rescue dog from the Navajo reservation] to the state park, if the weather permits, and continue my art in the afternoon."

Lapides is a member of the Jerome Artists Cooperative Gallery, the Northern Arizona Watercolor Society and the Sedona Arts Center, where she also shows her work.

ELLEN J.D. ROBERTS: LANDSCAPE AND STUDIO PAINTER

Jerome-based artist Ellen J.D. Roberts grew up in Chicago. "I was always an artist, from a very young age, always drawing. My mom would bring home reams of the old-style perforated edge computer paper, and I [would] fill it with art." Attending all public schools, she excelled and was soon placed in a program for gifted students.

In 1984, she was selected to attend the Young Artists program at the Art Institute of Chicago. She later won a scholarship to the University of Illinois's Chicago School of Art and Design, where she was immersed in an art scene of the late 1980s/early 1990s best described as a "Post Pop-Art Hangover." "My high school art teachers at Chicago's Lane Tech prepared me well for college and taught us a great variety of styles and purposes—commercial art, even graffiti art styles/stencils (limited to classroom, not actually put to use outdoors!), moviemaking, old-school color separation for print shop work, repurposing materials," she says. "For me, growing up reading *Mad Magazine*, satire and humor was a common theme in my young artwork, always light-hearted and often times trying to get a laugh." Two years later, she transferred to Northern Illinois University in DeKalb, where she completed her bachelor of fine arts in 1994.

She met her husband, Chad Roberts, in DeKalb, Illinois. He lived in the room below hers in an 1899 boarding home. "We called him 'the Mountain Biker Paul McCartney–looking guy.' Chad took me out into the forest and into nature. It was with him that this city girl made the big step to head west," she says.

The couple soon married in 1995 atop Starved Rock, overlooking the Illinois River. One month later, they were living in the various national forests of northern Arizona in a vintage pop-top camper. "We had done a trip to Arizona that spring of 1995, touring and camping in and around

Flagstaff, Sedona, Jerome, Prescott and decided that was the place we wanted to move. Arizona was just magic. It was all we could think about." By that year, they had Arizona driver's licenses and a Flagstaff P.O. box. "We lived in our vintage pop-top tent trailer in various parts of the forest until winter approached."

Ellen and Chad had fond feelings toward Jerome, so by Día de Los Muertos 1997, they had moved to a "tiny weird" apartment in Jerome. In 2001, they bought a historic brick bungalow in nearby Clarkdale that was built circa 1914. Ellen now works for the Verde Canyon Railroad as group coordinator in addition to her work as a quirky artist.

Although she is no longer a member of the Jerome Artists Cooperative, she still shows and sells her work in Jerome at Muttley Crue Co. Gallery near the post office, as well as at Rendezvous in Old Town (RIOT) in Cottonwood, Red Rooster Café in Cottonwood, the Clarkdale Caboose Gift Store in Clarkdale and Made Contemporary Crafts Gallery in Stinson Beach, California.

One of her most recent focuses is custom pet portraiture, a popular item. "As [the] owner of four dogs and a cat, I have developed a great knack for capturing the certain 'something' about them in art, as well as the pets of others." Mutley Crue, a dog-inspired boutique, has commissioned a series of breed portraits for their walls.

This artist is inspired by vintage film cameras and instant film photography, road trips, the vintage Volkswagens she owns; desert rivers, small-town life and the fantastic light of Arizona.

QIANG HUANG: STILL LIFE

Not many people can claim successful careers in both physics and art. But Qiang Huang, whose name is pronounced "Chong Wong," can do exactly that. Huang was born in 1959 and raised in Beijing, China, where he grew up watching his uncle draw and paint. Professionally trained, his uncle taught high school art in southern China and also worked for a city art program during the Cultural Revolution. Huang remembers "lots of propagandist-type art, like portraits of Mao Tse-Tung."

Huang's uncle would visit his grandma regularly in Beijing. He carried painting gear and liked to do plein-air paintings, remembers Huang. "I just watched him. Eventually I started writing letters to him and asked him to teach me art. So he showed me his art books and the basics of drawing." Huang also excelled in the limited art classes that were offered in his school—which were also related to communist themes.

After high school, Huang attended the University of Science and Technology of China in Hefei, Anhui Province, receiving a physics degree in 1982; then he worked for several years. In 1985, the University of Louisville in Kentucky offered him a scholarship for its master's program in physics. "China had just opened its doors, and not very many Chinese students came over. I didn't have any money at that time. I worked for the government, and everybody was equally poor, so I had no relatives or close friends to support me." After completing his master's degree, Huang knew he'd need a doctorate. He was accepted at the University of Alabama in Huntsville but was required to complete a second master's degree there toward his doctorate, which he earned in 1993. And all of these studies, of course, were conducted in English—his third language, after Chinese and Mandarin. Huang met and married his wife, Yuehong Song, in Huntsville, and then the couple moved to New Hampshire, where Huang joined a start-up company doing holography. Though the company eventually failed, Huang accepted a position in Austin with a high-tech optical company, where he currently works full time.

Reflecting on his dual career pursuits, Huang says his scientific background has some effect on his artwork: "It definitely makes me more sensitive about light. People think I'm doing two totally different things, but light unifies them. During the day I'm doing physical research on light, and the painting at night concentrates on the artistic representation of light. I'm constantly searching for the balance point between everything. I like to see my work as a balance between traditional and modern."

Huang paints mainly still life. Given his scientific background, it's no surprise that Huang makes masterful use of light in his paintings. His images gleam with rich, vibrant color and light. Oranges, apples and pears seem illuminated from within. Glass bottles, copper pots and ceramics glisten and glimmer with a life of their own. Blocky, Cézanne-like brush strokes add texture and charisma in such oils as *Now and Then*. "People say my style is very loose, simple, very painterly, like calligraphy," says Huang. "The reason I do still life is practical," he explains. "I have a day job, so that limits my painting time. When I paint flowers or an apple, I can design my composition and lighting, so there's lots of flexibility, and I have control. I pay lots of attention to shape, composition, light, value, and color."

Currently living in Texas (though teaching at the Sedona Arts Center), where "everything's big," Huang jokes. "There was a lot of empty wall space, and we were looking for artwork to decorate the new house." But Huang says he didn't like the art they could afford and couldn't afford the fine art he liked. "So I thought, why don't I do that myself?" When he began attending gallery receptions, he found much of the avant-garde artwork incomprehensible. Motivated, then, by both the practical and the philosophical, Huang set out to increase his knowledge. "I started taking workshops because I didn't have formal training," he says. One workshop was with the highly regarded figurative artist Scott Burdick. He also studied the works of and was inspired by late-nineteenth-century painters, including John Singer Sargent, Nicolai Fechin, William Bouguereau and Lawrence Alma-Tadema.

Gradually, Huang began to sell his work in galleries, as well as online. In fact, Huang says an important turning point came in 2007 when he started his popular "Daily Painter" blog. He produces a painting every weekday— sometimes on weekends as well—that he posts for sale online. He considers these daily paintings, which he creates in one to three hours, to be studies rather than completed projects. "I have something in mind that I want to practice. Then I write a comment on my blog and share my idea, experience and feelings," he says. "Most of the people buying my daily paintings are artists themselves. So they study the small paintings. I sell almost 100 percent of them."

Currently, Huang sells his larger paintings through galleries and the smaller ones online as well, keeping the two groups of work entirely separate. "The world is changing, and to be an artist, you must adapt to the current situation."

Huang is a signature member of the Oil Painters of America.

BERNIE LOPEZ: LANDSCAPE PAINTER

Jerome-based painter Bernie Lopez hails from San Diego, California. Lopez displayed an interest in the natural world around him as he was growing up. At an early age, he started sketching his observations and soon discovered his passion to create art.

Prior to becoming a full-time artist, Lopez worked in sheet metal fabrication, which might have something to do with the signature touch on his work. Like many artists, he was told he should consistently incorporate a stylistic element to render his work recognizable as his own. So with all his pieces, he paints a contemporary geometric border directly on the canvas—wide bands of neutral color to create a sense of contrast.

Lopez has three distinct series of acrylic paintings: the moonlight series, the sunset series and the landscape series, all inspired by visions of the American West. Rather than "photorealism," Lopez prefers to call his style "envisioned realism" because he doesn't work from photographs but pulls his imagery out of his memory and imagination: "It's what I see in my head." Like many painters, Lopez augments his supply of originals with high-quality prints to meet the demand for his work and make it more accessible to the public.

In his twenties, Lopez traveled around the western United States, absorbing the beauty that it offered. He visited Utah, Wyoming, Arizona and Colorado, stopping at all of the National Parks and forests along the way. Inspired by his journey, he became interested in landscape and abstract painting. Working with acrylics, Lopez began painting landscapes in a realistic style from his photographs. Throughout his artistic explorations, he continued to add abstractions to his paintings, combining a balance of natural landscapes, precise geometric elements and monochromatic colors.

Above all, he loves eliciting a reaction from views of his work. "I hope that it makes them feel good. That's the bottom line. That they feel peaceful and inspired to maybe try making art themselves or that it reminds them of something or somewhere they've seen, done or been. That's usually what I hear in response to my work…that it reminds them of something. One time this woman was standing here looking at *Aspens in the Snow*, crying. It affects everyone in a different way."

Today, Lopez resides in northern Arizona, where he works from his studio and home that he shares with his wife and three children. Lopez spends most of his time in the studio either painting or printing. "It is a great honor to belong to an artist community such as in Jerome with its eclectic and free style." Lopez's work is featured throughout the United States in both private and corporate collections as well as solo exhibitions in Arizona. Lopez did a commission for the Yavapai Indian tribe for the casino and many local Arizona collectors. "I have shipped artwork to many locations on the East Coast and as far north as Alaska…I am inspired by the natural beauty of Arizona; the diverse landscapes and unparalleled sunsets."

"To be an artist today requires the challenge of self-discipline and focus. You must consistently produce artwork and hope for the best. I focus my artwork on a feeling or mood and hoping that viewers will feel peaceful or even inspired. I think what keeps people coming to Arizona is the sense of freedom, open space and scenery. I know that's what keeps me here." Lopez is currently working on a fall aspen piece inspired by a recent trip to the Flagstaff-area mountains.

Lopez's work can be seen at the Jerome Artist's Cooperative Gallery.

JAN SITTS: MIXED MEDIA AND EXPERIMENTAL

I am attracted to mixed media for its endless possibilities; the adventure lies in not knowing where you are going—until you get there.

Although Jan Sitts has more than thirty years as an art instructor and professional painter, she enthusiastically continues her exploring and experimentation with many a medium. Sitts has worked in commercial art, public school teaching and international workshops. Using many materials, techniques, approaches to composition and emotion in creating a piece, Sitts has found her calling in mixed media. Her studies include the Kansas City Art Institute, a bachelor of arts degree at Western State College (Gunnison, Colorado) and ongoing workshops and seminars in the arts. She comments that "the beauty of Sedona and the artistic community...it draws. The art activities and galleries keep me in constant touch with my life's work." Sitts grew up in Kansas and knew she wanted to be an artist at the age of eight through her teachers' gentle but persistent encouragement.

Mixed media and exploratory techniques are not the terrain of the traditional painter, but students who journey with Sitts experience a "visual sensation" throughout the process "if they are able and willing to let go of old habits, break the paradigm," she says. Beginning the journey in mixed media requires an understanding of painting, mixing and layering colors, executing shapes by working with positive and negative space and nurturing an affinity for texture. "Once armed with knowledge of the fundamentals and of the possibilities of various media, creative spontaneity comes naturally. This continuous process of sustaining, validating and then reinventing is part of cultivating the creativity that nurtures our souls as food does our physical beings."

Throughout the years, Sitts has experimented with many design formats but the design she has come to favor over all others is the cruciform. "I have used this design in creating complex compositions through layering paper and exploring form with color and textures. I have always felt my spirituality plays an important part in my life's work, and I want to express this in my paintings." Collectors are looking for color and texture more than just a regular ho-hum realistic painting, she has observed. This is exactly what they find in abundance with Sitts's work.

One of Sitts's many collectors responded to the cruciform by saying, "The painting touched me deeply as in one strike of lightning I saw in the cross a symbol of every human life." If the outcome of a process becomes predictable, Sitts moves on to another sequence or approach. "Seldom do

I begin with a conscious idea. The idea emerges as the painting evolves. Making mixed media artworks is a feeling and joyful way to express my pleasure in the physical world with all its textures and colors."

Sitts's focus when she first moved to the region was Native American. Now she paints mainly desert scenes and other landscapes, such as Oak Creek canyon. "My most recent focus is on the beauty of abstraction that can be interpreted the way the viewer wants to see it." Sitts has grown in the past ten years from duplicating reality in her paintings to showing the "essence" of subjects in abstraction. "After living here for twenty eight years I have developed a large following in the community and throughout the country." In *Redstones*, Sitts, attracted by the landscape of Sedona, cut out individual paper pieces and applied them to the canvas to create the effect of "red stones."

To be an artist in contemporary times often means finding your style and continuing to develop. "This is a tremendous place for me. I have been blessed with much opportunity in the art world and throughout the country," says Sitts. Sitts now shows work in many galleries throughout the Verde Valley, including the VUE in Tlaquepaque in Sedona. Sitts is currently working on editorials and writing another book, as well as pleasing collectors with new and unique paintings for the gallery in Sedona.

JOHN M. SODERBERG: SCULPTOR

Prominent Sedona-based sculptor John Soderberg hails from a family of no small accomplishments. Soderberg's grandparents from both sides immigrated to America from Sweden and Denmark. Betty Lee, John's mother, studied ballet as a child and loved and encouraged the fine arts. His grandfather Joel Soderberg, a master carpenter, attended the Bible Institute of Los Angeles hoping to become a missionary to Africa. Being rejected numerous times by several missions due to his inadequate education, he offered his services as a carpenter-handyman to the African Inland Mission in 1914. He spent numerous years building church pews and various structures in several African countries from the Belgian Congo to Tanganyika and Kenya.

John's father, Richard, an avid oil painter, won first place in a Los Angeles–wide art competition at age seventeen. As a violinist, he even performed once with the Los Angeles Philharmonic. Richard attended UCLA and was class president. During World War II, he was an officer on a small navy ship headed up to the source of the Yangtze River in China. After his discharge, Richard returned to California for graduate work in civil engineering. While there, he and Betty Lee were married by Dr. Charles Fuller. As a child, John was deeply influenced by his father's storytelling and by his grandfather Joel's tremendous determination to serve in any way he could.

Richard and Betty left America with two-month-old David (John's eldest brother) and sailed to Manila less than two years after the end of World War II. They journeyed across India to Karachi and then took the night train to Peshawar. Bandits attacked the train and looted and killed at random. This was Betty's introduction to Afghanistan.

Richard Soderberg had been commissioned by Afghanistan's King Mohammed Zahir to be director of the country's first engineering school, the Afghan Institute of Technology. But upon reaching Kabul, the young couple was a bit dismayed to learn that the school was not yet in existence. Besides acting as director, Richard was expected to build it, staff it and equip it. He also had to perfect a means of teaching the prospective students English in a very short period of time, as there were no textbooks in Farsi. After much prayer and innovative hard work, the Afghan Institute of Technology was born.

Richard directed the school for some years, and he and Betty acted as undercover missionaries as well, as no missionaries were allowed in the country at that time. John spent his first five years of life in that country, and his first sculptures, commissioned by his mother, were executed in mud in the family's front yard. When he was five years old, the family left Afghanistan to live and work in India. The Afghans, to honor Richard and Betty, took the old Soderberg station wagon and mounted it on a concrete pedestal with a bronze plaque as a monument at the institute.

At age five in India, John began painting in oils with his father's paints and brushes. After living five years in that country, the family moved to Thailand, where John studied teakwood carving with the leading master, a Buddhist monk. The U.S. State Department was nervous about Americans living overseas "going native" and made it mandatory to visit America periodically. As a result, the Soderberg family traveled around the world every two and a half years, visiting churches, museums and galleries. Before graduating high school in Bangkok, Thailand, in 1967, John had circled the world eight times. He flew to America for college, but due to extreme culture shock, he ended up oil painting on the street in Berkeley, California, in the middle of the riots of the late 1960s. Not being very successful in his first professional art foray,

John M. Soderberg's *Merlin*. Patinaed bronze. *Courtesy of Sedona Chamber of Commerce & Tourism Bureau.*

he lived under a house on Telegraph Avenue and hid his canvases in a crack between two buildings. One night, at two o'clock in the morning, after going six days without food, he sold his masterwork—a large oil painting of a Buddhist monk and a candle—for two and a half dollars and bought six tacos. Eating his feast, contemplating his professional failure and considering the escalation of the riots and drug abuse around him, he decided to return to Southeast Asia. His only way of doing so was to join the U.S. Marine Corps in 1970. Though he spoke some Thai, taught martial arts and had eighteen years of experience overseas, the Marine Corps sent him to Yuma, Arizona, as an electronics/communication technician. "I was American but had never lived here in this country. Everything was different—clothing,

Top: John M. Soderberg. *Blue Deep*. Patinaed bronze. *Artist's collection.*

Right: John M. Soderberg. *Way of the Warrior*. Patinaed bronze. *Artist's collection.*

attitudes, food, music, etc. I had never seen TV and had no knowledge of what everyone took for granted—TV actors, common TV ads. I just felt very disconnected and alien. Just took a while to fit in, adjust to this new culture. I had, of course, been fitting in to new cultures most of my life—having lived or visited in many other countries."

After an honorable discharge, John spent time as a custom knife maker, a machinist and a gold and silver jeweler. He completed numerous commissions, including a bracelet for Elvis Presley, and made custom jewelry for individuals and service organizations. He evolved into a sculptor. He moved to Flagstaff, Arizona, with his wife and two baby daughters to learn the art of bronze. He worked in a small bronze art foundry for four years and sculpted his own work late into the night in his un-insulated chicken coop studio. After numerous starving-artist years, he ended up at Northern Arizona University as resident artist, where he later received his doctorate in humane letters. "In a painting, a novel, a symphony, the artist must create a whole, consistent world with backgrounds, actors, themes. In bronze, however, a whole world must be condensed into a single being. The piece must be infused, charged with meaning. John Soderberg's sculpture is poetry, in the full sense of the word," says author Paul Soderberg, his brother.

Soderberg has executed many monumental bronze commissions across the country, teaches at various art academies and nurtures and mentors many other sculptors. He has invented tools, materials and techniques that have bettered the world of art. In the late 1970s to early '80s, he invented "Classic Clay"—a superior modeling clay for sculptors. It never dries or cracks and has high tensile strength so little armature is needed, giving the sculptor more freedom of expression. It is used across the country and internationally now—including in Disneyland sculpture studios. Soderberg invented numerous tools for specialized sculpting, such as the eye tool for iris and pupil sculpting, and the sales technique used by many sculptors today called "precast sale price," which helps sculptors get their work out and start selling even if they don't have money for casting.

As a means of tithing and a way of giving back to his world, John has involved himself with service and charity work for thirty years. He has taught martial arts to disabled children and adults, given many sculpture workshops for children, served as a board member for domestic abuse shelters and other groups, worked on famine relief for the Tarahumara Indians in Mexico and was one of the original core members of Rancho Feliz, a charitable organization that builds and maintains orphanages and soup kitchens for kids and provides medical clinics to the poor, in addition to numerous other functions.

Among many others, Soderberg sculpted two bronzes for Amnesty International. One, the life-sized *Steve* (Steve Biko, from the film *Cry Freedom* with Denzel Washington), was in protest of the apartheid in South Africa. The other, *Steel Butterflies*, was in protest of the Soviet invasion and occupation of Afghanistan and the Soviets' widespread use of antipersonnel mines disguised as toys to target children. That piece was unveiled in Phoenix with Bob Hope and numerous celebrities during the Night for the Afghan War Orphans. Soderberg was chosen to sculpt the Freedom Award for an international group fighting contemporary slavery and human trafficking. Archbishop Desmond Tutu, Isabelle Allende and Demi Moore were among the notable presenters of the award to the recipients—those who had done the most to eradicate and expose modern slavery. John was knighted in the late 1990s by a Swedish count for service to women and children and for contributions to the world of art.

John lives and works in West Sedona, Arizona, in his art gallery/studio/classroom "Soderberg Bronze." His passion remains bronze, and his fascination is the lonely, timeless and ultimately noble drama of the human experience. He sculpturally explores worthy human themes in a manner that simply and honestly evokes empathy in the viewer.

"At this time, I am at work on two life-sized monuments and am waiting to start work on several larger-than-life bronzes."

MARK ROWND: ABSTRACT PAINTER

Soundscapes of Color and Light

The decision to be an artist was never really consciously made for abstract artist and musician Mark Rownd, whose art seems to have a melody all its own. "Growing up, I was just always trying to create something—whether it was playing music, drawing, painting—trying to build or invent something."

It never really stopped.

However, a career as an artist was very much a conscious decision. Rownd's formative years as an abstract painter began in the early 1970s as an art student at Rice University. The Abstract Expressionist movement was a major influence on his early exploration of formal elements of color, form and scale. Early influences in Rownd's abstract painting included the large-scale minimalist works of Barnett Newman, Mark Rothko and Clyfford Still.

In addition to painting, Mark experimented with minimalist forms of color, light and space in other disciplines as well, including photography, mixed media and music.

Deciding that life was too short not to follow what inspired him the most, regardless of the consequences, Rownd completed a bachelor of arts at Rice with a triple major in art and art history, psychology and sociology. Rownd continued to study large-scale abstract and color field painting with teacher and mentor Basilios Poulos. After a year of study and mentorship with Basilios, Mark returned to Rice to complete a fifth-year degree program for a BFA in art and art history with the arts scene in 1970s Houston as a vibrant backdrop. Galleries and jazz clubs were everywhere; the De Menils, whom some have called the Medicis of modern art, built a number of museums in the area and acquired a collection of art that has now reached seventeen thousand works. The environment was ripe for a lot of local talent to emerge. Rownd worked his way through college painting houses in the summer and playing music on the weekends.

Rownd began playing drums at the age of nine. After studying piano, Rownd began composing with electronic instruments in the early '80s, when the new technology was first introduced. "I became interested early on in the new composing tools available through computer technology," he said. Rownd was also one of the earliest adopters of new computer and music technology for composing and recording music back in the early '80s. "I used to hang out in Palo Alto, where it was all being created at the time, in the very earliest days of Apple/Mac and music technology development."

Rownd compares his composing technique to abstract painting. "As you start working on the blank canvas, soon the work begins to speak to you," he said. "Once you've created something that speaks on many levels, you've got a piece of art." Like painting, Rownd's music comes alive first as improvisations as he allows the energy and feelings of the moment extend into sounds. "The ideas express themselves," he said. "They sort of well up and then come out. Once you have established the beginning of a composition, then the piece itself starts telling you what to do next."

Rownd garnered international attention when he self-released his first work, *Desert Waves*, which he describes as embodying a contrast between very rhythmic and textural music. *Desert Waves* was placed on *New Age Voice Magazine*'s international airwaves charts. The artist garnered widespread acclaim from his second album, *Painting Twilight*, which was released through Spotted Peccary Music in 1998: "As a composer, Rownd has a distinct style of creating pieces that, much like the sounds in nature, flow together in ever-changing and unpredictable rhythms," reads commentary on the album's label.

The album—described as a textural, ambient, sublime work—earned Rownd the distinction of being named an Ambient Album of the Year finalist by *New Age Voice Magazine*. The magazine also placed the work as the number-four pick on its top fifty airwaves list. *Star's End*, *Wind and Wire Magazine* and *Exposé Magazine* all included *Painting Twilight* on their best of '98 lists.

While Rownd has performed many styles of music, especially jazz, on the drums, he was attracted to a minimalist approach to composing on piano, keyboards and electronics. "It was my interest in minimalist composers such as Steve Reich and John Adams that led me to an interest in ambient music," Rownd said. "Even though my background is in percussion originally, I became interested in 'minimalist' music, which I found to be very meditative, much like the spirit of ambient music."

Like the large-scale color abstract work that Rownd painted in college, sound fields with ambient textures and polyrhythmic percussion captivate him. The result is a unique sound that may be fully appreciated only by a deep listener of the work, as he produces rhythms that, according to some, rise out of the air like heat distortions. "I listen to the harmonic overtones as they present a melody that you haven't played," says Rownd of the way his music begins to take on a life of its own as he creates it.

Whether in music or art, Rownd is most inspired by improvisation and minimalism. Though he realizes it may sound incompatible, he has found that in order to improvise, you must have enough command of your skills to spontaneously compose in the moment. And to compose in the moment, you must be able to create without thinking. In other words, to spontaneously compose a piece of music, you can't be thinking about what to play. "It has to flow from within, without the interference of a thought process. It's the same with art. You can't be thinking about what to paint. You must just paint. And once a composition begins, whether it is art or music, you must be able to listen and hear what it's telling you comes next. So after the first stroke or note, it immediately begins to unfold. It's about listening, not thought or preconception," he remarks thoughtfully.

In spite of the seemingly wide variance of style, jazz improvisation or minimalist music can both embody the same process, much like the explosion of paint of a Jackson Pollock or the single color of a Barnett Newman. "I've always been most drawn to art or music which has little narrative or pictorial content. Rather it communicates something experientially through the elements of the composition itself. It makes you feel. On a spiritual level, rather than an emotional response or intellectual reaction based on content."

The light and color in Arizona are extraordinary, says Rownd. "And even in spite of the popularity of the region, there are still plenty of places where you are still more likely to encounter wildlife than a human." When it comes to presenting issues external to the art itself, Rownd has no agenda. His work is self-described as "just something to experience, like a single note of a glass bowl or an orchestra tuning up."

What are your goals in the next few years is a question I pose to the artist, but he doesn't think this way. "Life always seems to have another idea. But the simple answer is to do another painting. And write another piece of music." He does hope to never become comfortable in what he does—without that struggle to stay alive, art would cease to have its depth. Right now, Rownd is most proud of his next piece. "It's the joy of finding a new way to combine elements of color, form, light and space that you never quite happened upon before, that speaks something fresh to the spirit. "

Rownd's work has been featured in group shows and solo exhibitions in Los Angeles, San Diego, Phoenix, Houston and Sedona. His compositions have been featured on NPR, *Hearts of Space* and *Echoes*, and his music continues to receive airplay on satellite and digital radio, as well as be use in film and television.

Rownd's work can be seen at the Goldenstein Gallery in West Sedona.

JOELLA JEAN MAHONEY: PASSIONATE VISION

My paintings honor the earth. Painting is my lifelong work.

Born in Chicago, Illinois, Sedona resident Joella Jean Mahoney has been a committed artist since early childhood. "At age three, I experienced a powerful connection between myself and nature. I wanted to share this wonder at being alive with my parents and brothers. I could not yet explain wonder and awe in words, but I could through painting and drawing. So, I began serious art making and have never stopped."

Mahoney arrived in Flagstaff as a college student in 1951. The landscape of the region surrounding the little mountain town eventually provided the subject matter of her paintings. She fell in love with the broad vistas, great formations and intimate areas of the canyon land that make up the Colorado Plateau. Oak Creek Canyon and Sedona eventually became her home.

> *I saw Arizona for the first time in 1951 when I stepped off the train in Flagstaff to attend college. It was dawn. The stars overhead were like lanterns, the sky was crystalline and in the distance the mountains were like cardboard cutouts. The sun came up and turned the scene into Technicolor. That same day a friend took me on a drive through Oak Creek Canyon to the tiny town of Sedona. I had stepped into my future. I saw a landscape that matched how I felt inside.*

The colorful landforms and skies enhanced by the intense Arizona light have remained as an integral part of her works. Joella Jean paints the landscape outdoors following in the plein-air tradition. She then creates her large, rich and refined paintings in her Sedona studio, working with a fresh blank canvas and from a memory with no visual reference. Thus, her paintings express the experience of place, not just a picture of it.

Known for her dramatic, large-scale landscapes in oil, she also has a flower series, a figure series and a horse series, but the canyon landscape of the Colorado Plateau has become the major motif of her paintings. She was inspired by Giotto, Rembrandt, Mary Cassatt, Bay Area colorists, Abstract Expressionism, Richard Diebenkorn and Georgia O'Keefe. Artists today in Arizona, Mahoney sadly states, face the challenge of not being taken "seriously" back east. Even so, Mahoney developed her clientele over the years by dauntless hard work, perseverance and consistently making fine art. The wonder of the landscape holds her here, though she loves metropolitan areas as well. As a child, she was raised in both the grand museums of Chicago and the dune land lakeshore environment on Lake Michigan.

The Colorado Plateau landscapes contain all the elements of her huge originality: the spontaneous brush strokes, the inventive shapes, the incandescent color and the monumental scale of her work and vision. Mahoney's distinctive style bridges realism and abstraction while using color and structure to share with the viewer the spiritual content of experiencing the miracle of nature and life.

Passion and sensuality surface in the work of Joella Jean Mahoney. Her work is heated, expressive and spacious in decades when it has been hip to be cool, intellectual and minimal. She celebrated motifs from historic antiquity, presenting a life-affirming, spirit-rich present and envisioning the wealth of unfolding possible futures at a time when a future is hard to imagine and many contemporary artists are constructing throwaway art. She is a midcentury Expressionist who builds on the energy of Abstract Expressionism, the special examples of West Coast California painting.

In 1996, Mahoney was honored as distinguished alumnae by Northern Arizona University during its centennial year celebration. Her canvases are known internationally through the Art-in-Embassies Program from the U.S. State Department. Mahoney is listed in Phil and Marian Kovinick's *Encyclopedia of Women Artists* from the University of Texas Press.

Mahoney's landscape paintings have inspired many other painters. "My paintings have taught many people about the structure of art and the importance of color and shape," says Mahoney. "I see my influence in other's work."

According to Fred Duval, a former candidate for Arizona governor, "the paintings of Joella Jean Mahoney are to Northern Arizona what the paintings of Georgia O'Keeffe are to Northern New Mexico."

BILL NEBEKER: COWBOY ARTIST

It was 1978 in Phoenix at the Hyatt Hotel, also known as the day Bill Nebeker's work was deemed "good enough" to become a member of the highly selective group Cowboy Artists of America. "Merry [his wife] and I took the bronzes into their meeting room and then sat outside for a couple hours, worried to death and not knowing what to do if I got rejected or accepted. Then the door to the meeting room opened, and a tall man in a hat came over to us. The artist leaned down and grabbed Merry in a HUGE hug saying, 'I want to be the first to hug the wife of the newest member of the Cowboy Artists of America.'" With that, they were escorted into the meeting, and Bill sat among his artistic heroes, listening to the conversations and wondering, "What had I gotten myself into?" Unsure if he could live up to the standards of these great artists, who included John Clymer, Fritz White, James Boren and, of course, "the man" George Phippen.

Soon, Nebeker found himself hobnobbing with a who's who roster of celebrities who came to those early shows, including Barry Goldwater, Slim Pickens, Linda Grey (Dallas), George Montgomery, Johnnie Western and

Eddie Basha. Nebeker's greatest privilege, though, was riding and team roping with cowboy artists Joe Beeler, Fred Fellows, Bill Owen and Grant Speed, as well as many of the "real" working cowboys on the ranches. His artistic statement behind *The Legend Lives* reads:

> *The American Cowboy is unique to our nation's history. He came into existence at a pivotal time in our nation, after the great Civil War, driving cattle across great expanses of the West to the railheads going to the cities of the East. He worked and lived a lonely, independent, hard life. Myths grew out of the reality of his experiences to become the roots of our entire culture as books, films and then television brought him alive in the imagination of every American. Whatever he truly was in history, the cowboy is still very much alive today as he continues to gather, brand and ship cattle from the ranches he works on each day. They are fewer in number, but not in spirit.*

As a young boy, Nebeker made lots of toys with his hands and carved horses, guns, boats, boots and dogs but never thought of it as art. "I enjoyed three-dimensional things. My dad was a farmer and cowboy, and the only art I saw was of prints and calendars of Charlie Russell and Frederick Remington." As a teenager and then college student in the 1960s, Bill was not drawn to the counterculture movements, becoming instead enamored of the dress and lifestyles of the Old West. He tried rodeo in college and then purchased his own horse, learned to rope in local competitions and rode trails with his father, who had always worked with and owned horses as an "old-fashioned guy."

Nebeker was inspired by the art of George Phippen

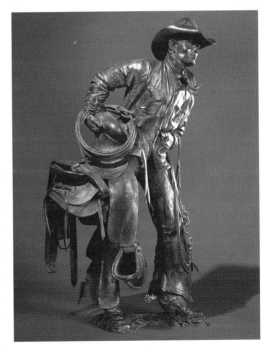

Bill Nebeker. *The Legend Lives.* Forty-seven by twenty by sixteen feet. 1988. *Artist's collection.*

Bill Nebeker. *Springin' the Trap*. Twenty-four by twenty by ten feet. 2012. *Artist's collection.*

and Charlie Russell to sculpt characters of the West that he knew and elements that he participated in personally with his rancher and cowboy friends. "They each portrayed the cowboys and lifestyles of their times, and I want to honor the ranchers and cowpunchers I have known and worked alongside, as I sculpt them." This "Code of the West" he greatly admires and attempts to emulate in his own life. Charlie Russell and Joe Beeler's historical Indian works, wet his whistle to begin researching many tribes. Nebeker has sculpted the Apache, Cheyenne, Crow, Comanche, Blackfoot, Pawnee, Ojibwa and Chippewa. "My main interest was in their weapons, clothing, accoutrements, culture and history of their famous battles and wars with the white settlers, Mexicans and other tribes, as well as their journey following the buffalo herds."

Long ago, Nebeker's parents asked Bill and then fiancée Merry to go with them to an art show in Prescott by the famous George Phippen. "The realism of cowboy paintings and sculptures took me back to the time of Indians, historic cattle drives and the old-fashioned values of God, country and family, which stood in such stark contrast to that current era in which I was so uncomfortable."

Perhaps these are some of the same reasons collectors love western art, Bill muses. "Many collectors of western art were raised on midwestern farms or ranches or, at the very least, had memories of visiting their grandparents' farms," explains Nebeker. "They rode horses, baled hay, worked hard, milked cows and herded sheep or milk cows." Almost all of the CAA member artists are conservative politically and ethically, as are most collectors of this genre of art. "It seems that those who keep the traditions, faith and work ethic of the Cowboy Way also buy cowboy art," he muses. Today though, Nebeker's sculptures are more often inspired by famous or historic lawmen, such as Wyatt Earp, and outlaws of that same era. Western films have also seeped into his artistic consciousness with portraits of John Wayne from *The Searchers* and Robert Duval from *Lonesome Dove*.

JOHN COLEMAN: SCULPTOR

His work is still, haunting and powerful. Southern California–born sculptor and cowboy artist John Coleman's art conveys the glory of history and community in the West. Down-to-earth John Coleman does not describe himself as a cowboy artist, however.

As the CAA became more prestigious, well-known illustrators became interested in western art, and some of the best were brought into the group, which gave the quality of the art a new dimension. "When I was brought into the Cowboy Artists of America, I mirrored Terpning's background, meaning that I was more illustrator than cowboy," says Coleman. "Howard Terpning is the leading working western artist in the country today, and I had always admired his work and the way he handles his subject matter, which is mostly Native American."

Coleman began his early art studies at the Art Center for Design in Los Angeles. Sculpting full time since 1994, John holds professional memberships in the National Sculpture Society and Cowboy Artists of America. He continues to study with other artists at the Scottsdale Artist School and in Colorado for anatomy. "I am a Fellow Member of the National Sculpture Society and member and past president of the Cowboy Artists of America. Although I may occasionally take a workshop, I'm better known for teaching them. I had an illustration job when I was still a teenager for a syndicated newspaper. Since then, I've always known I was going to be an artist."

Coleman's strong love of history in general is palpable during our interview. He has particular knowledge of Native American history with a focus on Montana and the Dakotas. Coleman is inspired by the West and is a mythology and history buff. "The Indian is the mythology of America, and I consider myself someone who paints the mythology of America." Coleman's art collectors say that they see life in his work; they feel the emotions he was trying to communicate. "To be able to get the story through" is important to Coleman. "The last thing I want to do is replicate objects, it's more of a metaphor...people might see their story in my art (the first rule of any artist) and to leave room for that."

"Since I'm outside of the culture, and I have virtually no idea what it would be like to be an Indian, I use my own experience and the native stories as a metaphor," says Coleman. Both a sculptor and a painter, his work is based on American mythology.

Coleman was attracted to Prescott because of the town's "western movie set" qualities with a strong ranching connection—the cowboy image was everywhere. "There is a lot of great art here, and it is a real easy place to be an artist. Prescott has a very large artist community, and the terrain lends itself to the subject matter that I'm most interested in, which is the American West."

The romantic in Coleman has always featured Native American history in his works. "People always have a tendency to react in a similar way to metaphor. It's really not about the story of the Indian but my own story through metaphors." He cites an Indian headdress piece as an example.

Coleman uses both human models and artifacts to work from, and most of his sculptures are based on historic description and museum collections. Coleman's personal favorite piece is titled *1876: Gall - Sitting Bull - Crazy Horse* and is based on the famous battle. While touring the Custer battle site, he said to himself, "Wouldn't it be interesting if the main participants in the battle came in to the studio to have their portraits done?" In this piece, they are all wearing and holding what they were during this momentous battle. "My work is based on historic description and artifacts found in museum collections."

Coleman completes about seven sculptures and between four and five paintings and drawings a year. Twenty years ago, would-be collector Howie Aper from Chicago bought a few pieces and became so taken with Coleman's work that he soon made a deal to purchase the number-one casting of each bronze sculpture edition. For the planned Museum of the West in Scottsdale opening in late December 2015, Aper generously has pledged his eighty-six sculptures of Coleman's work.

NANCY ROBB DUNST: INSTALLATION ARTIST

Nancy, a self-taught artist, has been creating art for thirty-two years in Arizona. Her work is three dimensional and incorporates fiber, wood, metal, polymers, glass and paint. She creates mosaics, mobiles, weavings and art installations. Although her medium changes depending on the requirements of the work, you can always recognize her work by the inclusion of some nature, some emotion, some text and strong color. *Southwest Art Magazine* writes, "While Dunst is sharply attuned to the classic elements and principles of design that govern good painting and sculpture, she is also free to push her versatile medium into numerous directions that free it." She has been commissioned by Sky Harbor International Airport in Phoenix, shown at the Phoenix Art Museum and was invited to the Biennale Internazionale Dell'Arte Contemporanea in Florence, Italy. Nancy was one of the first artists to receive the Sedona Project Grant from the Sedona Arts and Culture Commission.

While becoming an artist, Nancy was an associate professor on the faculty of Western International University in Phoenix and taught art, psychology, sociology and business. Nancy has a bachelor's degree in psychology, a master's degree in education and a master's degree in counseling. While teaching in 1974, she began creating and selling her art, an endeavor that developed into a small business that designed art for different corporate, municipal and private clients and employed nineteen people. She sold her business in the 1980s and moved north.

Having lived in Sedona for twelve years, she founded the Sedona Visual Artist Coalition, whose membership is now at over 170 artists. Nancy is very active in the arts and operates a summer art camp for children at the Sedona Creative Life Center. Having written about the arts for local papers and being a columnist for the *Art Talk Newspaper* (Scottsdale), she was asked to be a speaker at the Southwest Art Conference by Arizona Commission on the Arts.

I am exploring installation as an art form, and community issues as a subject. From a feminine prospective, in some of these works, I use slips and undergarments to suggest intimacy and the nakedness of inner thoughts close to the heart, continual thoughts that hang delicately from clotheslines and fragile branches asking the questions about the rest of one's life. In other works, I utilize found objects, and they use me in ways I never suspected.

5
PATRONS AND ARTISTS

In response to proposals to cut the arts to support England's war effort, Winston Churchill famously responded by saying, "Then what is it we are fighting for?" The presence of art in our lives is the one ray of hope in a contentious human experience. Art is a global communicator that transcends language and cultural barriers.

Artists in and of Sedona, often informally called a "City Animated by the Arts," take full advantage of the natural beauty and spirituality of their locale. There is an ever-present sense of community and appreciation for art here and an awareness of the artistic process that the general population of the area appreciates and supports. But no artist can exist without the support of a patron in some form.

The relationship between artist and patron is a lengthy and ever evolving one. Patronage was practiced as a social institution throughout early modern Europe, peaking somewhere between the fourteenth and seventeenth centuries. It is nearly impossible, however, to determine a specific origin of the tradition. By nature, it developed very gradually over long periods of time as different families and individuals rose and diminished in prominence in their respective corners of the world.

Historically, few artists have been able to work exclusively on their own without thought or care as to whether they will find favor with patrons. In the early Renaissance, the patronage of one of the noble courts or the Catholic Church was the vital framework within which an artist was obliged to operate. Leonardo de Vinci worked for many years for a variety of patrons not just as a painter but also in his other incarnations as architect, engineer, inventor and philosopher. Great monarchs, such as Louis XIV, used art and the work of contemporary artists to increase their prestige and political standing. The papacy employed art to spread Christianity and to promote the Catholic Church's worldly power and influence.

Without these influential patrons, it is clear that the greatest artists of the seventeenth century would not and could not have created their masterpieces. However, it was in seventeenth-century Holland that collecting the work of living artists for private commercial reasons as well as for pleasure first began.

The eighteenth and early nineteenth centuries saw a golden age for the private collector. During this time, many great masterpieces of antiquity and the Renaissance were taken from their original settings and sold to foreign art collectors. The modern picture dealer came into prominence in the early nineteenth century when many of the famous firms that are still in existence today were founded. As the artist found greater freedom to express a personal vision rather than one that was shared with or initiated by a patron, these dealers became a very necessary intermediary between the painter and collector. Indeed, without the courage of a few intrepid dealers and collectors, the Impressionists and the great masters of the Modern movement, such as Picasso, Matisse, Modigliani and Pollock, would have faced extraordinary financial difficulties and lacked an indispensable source of support for their work.

Today, artists are extremely fortunate to have a freedom not very common in the history of art. Royalty and the church were the only buyers in the art world of previous centuries; the artist of modern times is free to paint whatever he or she desires, knowing that, somewhere, there is an audience for the work.

Richard and Vicki Van House exemplify the devoted modern-day collector as collectors of art over the course of their entire lives. "I purchased my first original art—two seascape watercolor paintings by James Ashcroft—in the late 1960s at the Ann Arbor Street Fair in Ann Arbor, Michigan," remembers Richard, who lived in Australia in the late 1980s and spent quite a bit of time traveling around the country collecting original Australian landscapes. "When I moved back to the United States, I took my son, who was then ten years old and hadn't seen much of America, to many of the western national parks, and that stimulated my interest in Native American and western American art. The art collecting disease continued from there," he says. "I purchased my first western American original painting—*Trap Thieves* by Robert Duncan—in 1991.

Since Vickie and I have been together, her more contemporary art interests have resulted in our collection becoming a bit more varied and eclectic. We have downsized our collection, though, as a result of moving from our home to two condos in Ann Arbor and Scottsdale."

The Van Houses have a large and varied art collection that includes Grand Canyon landscapes and other western American paintings; European paintings; a number of paintings by present and former members of the Cowboy Artists of America (CAA); wildlife paintings; city scenes; several paintings from local Ann Arbor, Michigan artists; nocturnal scenes; and figurative works. They presently own thirteen paintings by Sedona-based artist Curt Walters. One of Curt's paintings, titled *Deliquescence* (a painting of snowy Oak Creek Canyon in Sedona, Arizona), is one of the Van Houses' favorites. Coincidentally, the Van Houses also own a home in Sedona. Thus began a great friendship. Curt painted the couple in the forefront of his larger painting of the Las Vegas Strip titled *Contradictions*, which was included in the June 2014 Prix de West show.

In certain locales artists are admittedly more blessed than others, and Sedona is one of those. With more visual and performing artists (many of them internationally recognized) than most towns of its size, one of the highest per capita amounts of emerging artists and over forty art galleries and an active gallery associations, Sedona and the Verde Valley have received much support for their collectors, dealers, patrons and various institutions over the years.

"Many of these people, myself included, moved here because we got zapped with Red Rock Fever. That's what Sedona does," says Julee Cohen, president of the Sedona Visual Artists' Coalition. "Sedona brings out the creative spirit in people who never thought they could draw a straight line. People take a class at the Sedona Arts Center or a workshop in town, they find their muse and their art careers are launched."

Art organizations in Sedona provide a support system for creativity and camaraderie. There's a little for everyone. The Sedona Camera Club caters to photographers; the Northern Arizona Watercolor Society is an avenue for water media artists. The Pastel Society ministers to pastel artists. The Sedona Arts Center is a major hub for artists and poets as well. The Sedona Arts Festival creates a yearly venue for arts enthusiasts, and the Sedona Visual Artists' Coalition sponsors a thriving Open Studio Tour, all amounting to the continual assertion by all professionals involved that "Sedona is a family of artists." "Sedona is a community that truly enhances the arts and believes in the impact that artists make in the world," says Cohen. "Local businesses generously donate funds to our endeavors without batting an eye."

This support for the arts comes from varied organizations, as well, including the Sedona Public Library, one of the small percent of non-tax-supported libraries in the country, located in a beautiful Old Sedona structure shaded by pine. The library's mission aligns with the goals of the Sedona artist community, and it serves as a central location for Sedona's artists to display their art, teach art and research various techniques through a collection of art-related books and articles. The library has designated a permanent liaison to both the Sedona Art Center and the proposed Sedona Art Museum.

Through its Rotating Artist Program, a different artist is showcased each month. Publicity is widespread throughout the Verde Valley for these events; the library showcases a variety of media, including oil paintings, photography, decorative and useable quilts, watercolors, nail sculptures, Sedona Red Rock High School student art, glass art, embroidery, "spirit wood" carvings, astrophotography, found art assemblage and wearable art. Among the many art projects on permanent display are a bronze statue, *Sedona Miller Schnebly*, by Susan Kliewer and mixed-media piece *Of Fears and Dreams…American Priorities Visited* by forty-five Sedona Red Rock High School art students under the direction of artist Nancy Dunst.

But the bulk of support, financial and otherwise, to the area's artists still comes from the galleries and their owners. Of the one to two hundred art galleries functioning in town, the most charismatic is the Goldenstein Gallery located in quiet west Sedona, across from the Sedona public library. Many patrons come to an art gallery specifically to support artists. Talking with vivacious and gracious gallery owner and art patron herself Linda Goldstein is a treat; she holds nothing back and can inspire even the most cynical with her dedication to and belief in the power of art.

Linda is a native of the Sedona Verde Valley, a rarity. "Artists and others become so interested by the incredible scenic beauty, something that is so deeply inspiring about the town…The town is so small but big things happen here to this day," she says. One such example is the organization Gardens of Humanity started in Sedona by a local artist Adele Seronde. "The town really touches people in a loving and inspirational way. So many artists in the early part of the century were women, and this is highly unusual." This, she theorizes, influences the town's vibe being softer, having a kind of "woman's touch" almost.

Linda's eclectic gallery works with over sixty artists who mainly reside in Sedona and throughout northern Arizona. Over the years, she has represented Kevin McCarthy, Mike Meadow and pointillist painter Sherab Khandro. Though their mediums and materials vary dramatically, one thing they all share is this idea of embracing their "southwestern-ness."

A passionate business owner to boot, Linda was working in a gallery in Santa Fe when she fell in love with artists as people. She still is moved in remembering how "patrons of art are doing what they do to better their surroundings. There are those who create and those who appreciate; it is a very symbiotic circle. The patrons of today collect what enhances their life; the piece will be with them during holidays, birthdays and private moments. It comes back full circle in seeing its artist grow."

PEGGY GUGGENHEIM

MODERN ART'S GREAT BENEFACTRESS

An heiress to the Guggenheim mining fortune, Peggy Guggenheim was an intriguing, eccentric figure in the world of art (her father, Benjamin Guggenheim, went down with the *Titanic*). Far from being a frivolous socialite, the New York–born Peggy Guggenheim became a devoted patron of artists and was one of the most influential figures in the history of twentieth-century art. After years spent in Europe collecting the likes of Kandinsky and Duchamp, Guggenheim returned to New York in 1941 and opened the groundbreaking Art of This Century Gallery on West Fifty-seventh Street. The gallery was dedicated to Cubist, Abstract, Surrealist and Kinetic art. There she fostered the careers of several promising artists, including Pollock and Ernst. She later lived comfortably but simply in an unfinished eighteenth-century palace in Venice that had fallen into disrepair. Now the Peggy Guggenheim Collection—which features works from early Picasso; Surrealists Ernst, Dalí and Magritte; and Abstract Expressionists, such as Jackson Pollock, many of whom she championed before they were fashionable—is Italy's number-one museum of modern art. Before her death, she donated the more than three hundred masterpieces and the palazzo to the Solomon R. Guggenheim Foundation (Solomon was Peggy's uncle), which also owns and operates the Guggenheim Museum in Frank Lloyd Wright's famous spiral building in New York, as well as Frank Gehry's spectacular Guggenheim Museum in Bilbao, Spain. She died at the age of eighty-one in 1979.

We discuss art's ability to restore the human spirit often from places of utter despair. During her gallery's public exhibitions, collectors often share with the artists what their painting meant for them. "A gentleman who lost his child was able to go on after looking at this particular piece of art. What else in our society can touch our hearts so readily?" she pointedly asks. Patrons are truly the unsung heroes of the art world, and Linda is most definitely among them. "They understand that the arts are so critically important to society," she says. "We need them more than ever."

AFTERWORD

"I'm not going to museums. The pictures spook me out."
—*Woody Allen in* Small Time Crooks

There is no doubt that the future of the art community in the Verde Valley is ripe with promise. This is after all a place rich in history with artists whose work is often more recognized elsewhere than here. Many in this community of artists hope that in the future there will be more public exhibition spaces for the art being created in the area. This will aid in giving recognition to the art history of the artists who lived and worked here in the past as well. Additionally, an art museum would be an important step forward for the community.

The town's arts scene holds the good, the bad and the uncertain. Though the town itself is consistently rated a top arts destination, Santa Fe, in contrast, is built on the reputation of Georgia O'Keefe. Sedona has no equivalent. Visitors flock to Sedona primarily for the red rock splendor and, in the case of Arizonans, as an escape from the desert heat as much or more than for its reputation as an arts destination. The city's galleries have in some circles a reputation for being too stuck in the mindset of regional art. Many local artists feel the city of Sedona has not been supportive of the arts, choosing to focus more on jeep rides and motels. Indeed, Sedona receives three times the tourists of Taos and Santa Fe who buy only a fraction of the art available in town. Local artists who are based in Sedona often do not show their work in town because of this—exhibiting instead in places like Carmel, Santa Fe and New York.

But there is much to come. Each year, Sedona is competing with other cities that are also top arts destinations; it has not gone unnoticed that these other cities all have art museums. "If Sedona is to maintain its place as a world-class arts destination it simply must have an art museum, which has been shown to contribute to visitors wanting to be in the city," comments John Oaks, the Sedona Art Museum's president. The planned nonprofit Sedona Art Museum may change all that. There are ambitious plans to acquire art from the Verde Valley of both famous and contemporary artists of the area and to present educational programs to teach the community about the cultural heritage of the area and what is current in art.

A Guide to the Galleries

ALT GALLERY
671 State Route 179, Suite AST-5
Sedona, Arizona 86336
928.554.7840
www.altgallerysedona.com
Antique, vintage and estate fine art; rare and out-of-print books, artifacts
and collectibles; authorized dealer for "The Art of Dr. Seuss"

ANDERSON/MANDETTE GALLERY
P.O. Box 866
Jerome, Arizona 86331
928. 634.3438
robinj@sedona.net
www.anderson-mandette.com
Portraits, sculpture, drawings, landscapes and short stories by Robin John
Anderson and Margo Mandette

ANDREA SMITH GALLERY
Tlaquepaque
336 Highway 179
Sedona, Arizona 86336
888.644.5444
info@andreasmithgallery.com
www.andreasmithgallery.com
Original paintings, limited-edition prints by world peace artist Andrea Smith
and sacred art

THE CODY DELONG STUDIO
300 Hull Avenue
Jerome, Arizona 86331
928.300.4576
cody@codydelong.com
www.codydelong.com
Originally a Studebaker dealership during the town's mining days; owned by artist Cody DeLong; features oils, landscapes and prints

EXPOSURES INTERNATIONAL GALLERY OF FINE ART
561 State Route 179
Sedona, Arizona 86336
928.282.1125
artists@exposuresfineart.com.
www.exposuresfineart.com
Sculpture, painting, photography and glass

GALLERY 527
527 Main Street
Jerome, Arizona 86331
928 649 2277
www.gallery527jerome.com
Painting, sculpture, ceramics, fused glass, jewelry and photography

GALLERY OF MODERN MASTERS
671 State Route 179
Sedona, Arizona 86336
928.282.3313
info@galleryofmodernmasters.com
www.galleryofmodernmasters.com
Glass art, oils, original lithographs, sculptures, ceramics, glass and photography by local artists, regional and international artists, including masters from Picasso and Chagall

GOLDENSTEIN GALLERY
70 Dry Creek Road
Sedona, Arizona 86336
928. 204.1765
info@goldensteinart.com
www.goldensteinart.com
Painting, sculpture, fine furniture, jewelry, Judaica, multimedia, photography, pottery, woodwork, fiber and gourd art

HONSHIN FINE ART
336 Highway 179
Sedona, Arizona 86336
928.282.0709
Insight@HomshinFineArt.com
www.honshinfineart.com
Local art reflecting the beauty of nature in a fusion of Eastern and Western perennial spiritual tradition

KUIVATO GLASS GALLERY
336 Highway 179, Tlaquepaque Suite B-125
Sedona, Arizona 86339
928.282.1212
kuivato@esedona.net
www.kuivatoglassgallery.com
Art glass, jewelry and light sculptures

LANNING GALLERY
431 State Route 179, A1-2
Sedona, Arizona 86336
928.282.6865
mail@lanninggallery.com
www.lanninggallery.com
Original oils; acrylics; exceptional sculpture; handmade, hand-painted furniture; and distinctive jewelry by world-renowned and cutting-edge emerging artists

MOUNTAIN TRAILS GALLERIES
336 SR 179, Suite A-201
Sedona, Arizona 86336
928.282.3225
fineart@mountaintrails.com
www.mountaintrails.com
Western and Southwestern painting and sculpture

RENEE TAYLOR GALLERY
336 Highway 179
Sedona, Arizona 86339
928. 282.7130
www.reneetaylorgallery.com
Contemporary fine art in metal, canvas and multimedia formats

ROWE FINE ART GALLERY
336 SR 179, Suite A-102
Sedona, Arizona 86336
928.282.8877
info@rowegallery.com
www.rowegallery.com
Contemporary and traditional southwestern paintings and bronze sculptures

SEDONA ARTS CENTER
15 Art Barn Road
Sedona, Arizona 86336
928.282.3865
sac@sedonaartscenter.org
www.sedonaartscenter.org
Painting, drawing, sculpture, ceramics and mixed media

SODERBERG BRONZE
1370 West Highway 89A, Suite 16
Sedona, Arizona 86336
928.567.6341
www.johnsoderberg.com

TLAQUEPAQUE ARTS & CRAFTS VILLAGE
336 State Route 179
Sedona, Arizona 86339
928.282.4838
info@tlaq.com
www.tlaq.com

ZEN MOUNTAIN GALLERY
515 Main Street
Jerome, Arizona 86331
928.634.5009
www.zenmountaingallery.com
Contemplative and contemporary fine art, jewelry, pottery and photography

BIBLIOGRAPHY

Bowers, Ty. *Excellence by Design: A Visual History of Public Art in Oro Valley, Arizona.* Tucson, AZ: Alliance, 2009.

Carr, Betty. Personal interview, September 5, 2014.

Carr, Howard. Personal interview, June 23, 2014.

Chesler, Donna. Personal interview, November 22, 2014.

Cohen, Julee. Personal interview, November 20, 2014.

Coleman, John. Personal interview, September 29, 2014.

DeLong, Cody. Personal interview, August 22, 2014.

Faerna, José M. *Ernst.* New York: Harry N. Abrams, 1997.

Fahlman, Betsy. *The Cowboy's Dream: The Mythic Life and Art of Lon Megargee.* Wickenburg, AZ: Desert Caballeros Western Museum, 2002.

———. *New Deal Art in Arizona.* Tucson: University of Arizona Press, 2009.

Fillmore, Gary. *Shadows on the Mesa: Artists of the Painted Desert and Beyond.* Atglen, PA: Schiffer Publishing, 2012.

Fisher, Leonard Everett. *Remington and Russell.* New York: Gallery Books, 1985.

Gianelli, Sarah. "As the Day Falls to Night: Landscapes of the Imagination." *Noise Arts & News,* June 2014.

Glenn, Reed. "Seeing the Light." *Southwest Art,* February 15, 2011.

Goldstein, Linda. Personal interview, June 25, 2014.

Hagerty, Donald J. *Leading the West.* Flagstaff, AZ: Northland Publishing, 1997.

Hedgpeth, Don. "History." http://www.cowboyartistsofamerica.com.

———. *Joe Beeler: Life of a Cowboy Artist.* Vail, CO: Diamond Tail Press, 2004.

Hoag, Betty. Oral history interview with Eugenia Everett, October 14, 1964. Archives of American Art's New Deal and the Arts Oral History Project.

Huang, Quang. Personal interview, November 8, 2014.

James, Nancy. *The Artists' Arizona: A Book of Days.* Tucson, AZ: Paseo Fine Arts, 1988.

Lapides, Birgitta. Personal interview, June 28, 2014.

Lopez, Bernie. Personal interview, July 2, 2014.

Mahoney, Joella Jean. Personal interview, September 25, 2014.

Nebeker, Bill. Personal interview, July 25, 2014.

Negri, Sam. *Art in Arizona*. Tucson, AZ: Stanbery Corporation, 1994.

Oakes, John. Personal interview. September 14, 2014.

Parks, Stephen. "The Greatest Subject on Earth." *Southwest Profile*, February 1989.

Phippen, George. *The Life of a Cowboy: Told Through the Drawings, Paintings, and Bronzes of George Phippen*. Tucson: University of Arizona Press, 1969

Powell, Lawrence P. "Letter from the Southwest." *Westways*, August 1978.

Rapaport, Diane S. *Home Sweet Jerome: Death and Rebirth of Arizona's Richest Copper Mining City*. Boulder, CO: Johnson Books, 2014.

————. Personal interview, May 15, 2014.

Reynolds, Catherine A. *Cowboy Artists of America*. El Paso, TX: Desert Hawk Publishing, 1988.

Roberts, Ellen J.D. Personal interview, May 20, 2014.

Rooney, Ashley E. *Contemporary Art of the Southwest*. Atglen, PA: Schiffer Publishing, 2013.

Rownd, Mark. Personal interview, June 22, 2014.

Russell, John. "From Max Ernst, for Your Eyes Only." *New York Times*, February 24, 1991.

Santillanes, Dave. Personal interview, August 24, 2014.

Sarda, Michel F. *Faces of Arizona: A Tribute to Artists and Art Patrons of Arizona*. Phoenix, AZ: Art Renaissance Initiative, 1999.

Sedona Arts Center. "History." http://www.sedonaartscenter.com.

Sidy, Richard. Personal interview, September 8, 2014.

Sitts, Jan. Personal interview, May 27, 2014.

Soderberg, John. Personal interview, June 7, 2014.

Stroud, Isabel M. *Sedona Heritage: Arizona Artists*. Sedona, AZ: Saru Press International, 1997.

Tanning, Dorothea. *Birthday*. Santa Monica, CA: Lapis Press, 1987.

Troccoli, Joan C. *Painters and the American West: The Anschutz Collection*. Denver, CO: Denver Art Museum; New Haven: Yale University Press, 2000.

Wagner, Margaret E. *Maxfield Parrish & the Illustrators of the Golden Age*. San Francisco, CA: Pomegranate, 2000.

Walters, Curt. Personal interview, October 26, 2014.

Watson, Bruce. "Beyond the Blue: The Art of Maxfield Parrish." *Smithsonian Magazine*, July 1999.

Wood, Harry. "Egyptian Sculptor Carves Serenity in Onyx Stones." *Scottsdale Daily Progress*, June 13, 1975.

INDEX

A

Abstract 8, 9, 58, 59, 69, 83, 99
Abstract Expressionism 24, 25
acrylic 76
American art 18, 22, 23, 25, 42, 59, 96
American West 20, 21, 25, 41, 76,
        92, 108
Arcosanti 45
Arizona Territory 19

B

Ball, Lucille 14, 15
Beeler, Joe 41, 57, 58, 89, 91
Broken Arrow 35
bronze 9, 21, 28, 43, 55, 59, 60, 61,
        79, 80, 81, 82, 83, 93, 98, 106

C

Carr, Betty 5, 65–67
Carr, Howard 5, 67–68
Chagall, Marc 29, 31
Chapel of the Holy Cross 12, 13
Churchill, Winston 95

Clarkdale 44, 73
Coleman, John 5, 9, 91–93
collage 30, 70, 71
color field painting 58, 59, 84
Cottonwood 32, 67, 73
cowboy art 41, 91
Cowboy Artists of America 40, 41, 42,
        43, 88, 91, 92, 97, 108

D

Dada 28, 29, 30, 33, 35
Dalí, Salvador 28, 30, 31, 99
da Vinci, Leonardo 66
de Kooning, Willem 24
DeLong, Cody 5, 68–69
Dixon, Lafayette Maynard 23
Doublemint twins 15
Duchamp, Marchel 29, 31, 99
Dunst, Nancy Robb 57

E

Europe 12, 18, 21, 22, 24, 29, 31, 95
Everett, Eugenia 55–57

F

Fitzgerald, F. Scott 53
Frankenthaler, Helen 58–59

G

gardens 16, 35, 49
Gardens of Humanity 98
Gobran, Nassan 33, 34, 35, 36, 38, 40
Goldwater, Barry 12, 88
Grand Canyon 19, 20, 21, 22, 23, 25,
    27, 54, 63, 64, 65, 69, 97
Great Depression 23
Grey, Zane 21, 88
Guggenheim, Peggy 8, 31, 32, 99

H

Holland 96
Hollywood 15, 54
House of Seven Arches 14–16
Huang, Qiang 5, 73–75

I

illustration 20, 50, 51, 92
Impressionism 18
Impressionists 41, 96
installation 93

J

Jerome 2, 5, 24, 44, 45, 46, 47, 67, 68,
    69, 71, 72, 73, 75, 76, 103, 104,
    106, 108

K

Kliewer, Susan 98

L

landscape 8, 9, 17, 19, 20, 22, 23, 24,
    25, 33, 51, 53, 54, 62, 63, 65,
    67, 69, 70, 71, 76, 78
landscape painting 17, 19, 20, 69
Lapides, Birgitta 69–72

Lewis and Clark Expedition 18
Lopez, Bernie 5, 75–76

M

Mahoney, Joella Jean 5, 10,
    86–88, 108
Megargee, Lon 22, 53–54
Mexico 13, 19, 21, 44, 59, 61, 82
Miller, Abe 13, 14
mixed media 77
modernism 41
Montana 21, 92
Moran, Thomas 19, 20, 21, 22
mural 7, 14, 22, 23, 49, 52
muralist 23

N

Native Americans 18, 19
Nebeker, Bill 5, 43, 88–91
New Mexico 11, 18, 21, 22, 42, 54,
    64, 68
New York 7, 15, 21, 23, 24, 29, 31, 32,
    35, 41, 45, 50, 52, 62, 64, 65,
    67, 70, 71, 99, 101, 107, 108

O

Oak Creek Canyon 15, 35, 97
Oak Creek Tavern 41
oil 20, 42, 62, 70, 78, 79, 81, 98
O'Keefe, Georgia 101
Oregon Territory 18

P

Parrish, Maxfield 9, 49–53
patrons 45, 95, 96, 98, 99
Philadelphia 20, 45, 50, 54
Phippen, George 41, 42, 88, 89, 91
pioneers 27
plein-air 17, 18, 63, 67, 68, 69, 73
Pollock, Jackson 8, 9, 24, 25, 32, 59,
    85, 96
Powell, John W. 19, 20

R

Remington, Frederick 21, 41, 53, 89, 107
Renaissance 15, 66, 95, 96, 108
Roberts, Ellen J.D. 5, 72–73
rock art 9, 24, 27, 49
Roosevelt, Theodore 21
Rownd, Mark 5, 8, 9, 83–86
Russell, Charles M. 21, 41, 53, 89, 90, 91

S

San Diego 19, 55, 75, 86
Santa Fe Railway 22
Santa Fe Trail 18
Santillanes, Dave 5, 62–63
sculptors 55, 59, 78, 91, 108
Sedona Arts Center 8, 13, 35, 36, 38, 47, 55, 72, 74, 97, 106, 108
Sedona Public Library 5, 98
Sedona Visual Artist Coalition 93
Seronde, Adele 16, 98
Sitts, Jan 5, 9, 77–78
Soderberg, John M. 5, 78–83
Stanley, John Mix 19, 20
Staude, Marguerite Brunswig 12
still lifes 66, 74
studio 61, 68, 72, 97
Surrealism 25, 28, 30, 35

T

Tanning, Dorothea 8, 9, 24, 28, 32, 34
Taos 11, 44, 54, 101
Tlaquepaque Arts and Crafts Village 13–14
tourism 16, 37, 39, 40, 43, 56, 80

V

Verde Valley 9, 27, 44, 45, 46, 47, 59, 60, 63, 68, 69, 78, 97, 98, 101, 102
Vermont 52, 71

W

Waddell, John Henry 5, 59–62
Walters, Curt 5, 63–65, 97
watercolor 7, 42, 65, 96
western art 9, 41, 44, 58, 64, 91
World War I 22, 29, 30
World War II 28, 31, 35, 42, 79
Wright, Frank Lloyd 11, 23, 99

ABOUT THE AUTHOR

Lili DeBarbieri is a noted author and librarian. Lili's other books include *Location Filming in Arizona* and travel narrative *A Guide to Southern Arizona's Historic Farms and Ranches*, both finalists in the New Mexico–Arizona Book Awards. She also has a forthcoming children's picture book, *Sand Dune Daisy: A Pocket Mouse Tale*. Her work continues to be featured in a diverse range of publications, including Amazon bestseller *The Utah Prairie Dog* and *Mighty Colorado*, as well as in the new television series *Film in Arizona*. Lili currently serves as a grants panelist at the Arizona Commission on the Arts. Originally from Philadelphia, she calls Tucson home and can be found working on a fledgling young adult suspense novel, among her many other endeavors.